ARMOURED HUSSARS VOLUME 1

Images of the 1st Polish Armoured Division 1939-47

Janusz Jarzembowski

Helion & Company

Helion & Company Limited
26 Willow Road
Solihull
West Midlands
B91 1UE
England
Tel. 0121 705 3393
Fax 0121 711 4075
Email: info@helion.co.uk
Website: www.helion.co.uk
Twitter: @helionbooks
Visit our blog http://blog.helion.co.uk/

Published by Helion & Company 2014. Reprinted with corrections 2016
Designed and typeset by Mach 3 Solutions Ltd (www.mach3solutions.co.uk)
Cover designed by Farr out Publications, Wokingham, Berkshire
Printed by Hobbs The Printers Ltd, Totton, Hampshire

Text and images © Janusz Jarzembowski

ISBN 978 1 909384 43 9

British Library Cataloguing-in-Publication Data.
A catalogue record for this book is available from the British Library.

All rights reserved. No part of this publication may be reproduced, stored in a retrieval system, or transmitted, in any form, or by any means, electronic, mechanical, photocopying, recording or otherwise, without the express written consent of Helion & Company Limited.

Front cover – Polish Battle group with Sherman Mk IIAs approaching Wilhelmshaven, 06 May, 1945, led by Major Gutowski, CO 2nd Armoured Regiment (page 111, captions 200-220); (top left) – Poland shoulder title worn on both sleeves of the British Army issue uniform; (bottom right) – 1st Polish Armoured Division formation sign sleeve patch, February 1942, worn on the left sleeve of the British Army issue uniform, designed by Captain Stanisław Glaser, 10th Dragoons Regiment.

Rear cover, from top, starting left to right: 1. Train ticket, Bucharest, Romania, dated 10 December 1939; 2. Certificate for Aleksander Jarzembowski, France, 1940 (page 18, caption 13); 3. Join the Polish Army in Canada, pamphlet, circa 1942 (page 49, captions 76-77); 4. Photo, German prisoners, Rhede, Germany, 1945 (page 97, caption 172); 5. 1st Polish Armoured Division commemorative cross, established London, 10 April 1985 by the association of veterans for the ex-soldiers of the Division; 6. Honorary insignia, Beveren-Waas, Belgium, 1946 (page 130, caption 235); 7. Metal Armoured Forces badge; 8. Photo, Colour Party, 2nd Armoured Regiment, Herzlake, Germany, 1946 (page 134, captions 244-249); 9 & 10. Front and reverse of commemorative card for the Polish 16th Tank Brigade, Scotland, 1943 (page 33, captions 42-43); 11. Post-war Divisional pin; 12. British issue kit belonging to A.L.Jarzembowski, helmet, beret, tank oversuit, nicknamed the 'Pixie Suit', belt with holster and map case; 13. British Battledress uniform and accessories belonging to A.L.Jarzembowski; 14. Photo, Sherman tank of Lieutenant Colonel Stanisław Koszutski (left in turret) 2nd Armoured Regiment, Germany, April 1945; 15. Polish National Eagle (metal) cap badge; 16. 16th Tank Brigade shoulder patch, Scotland 1941(page 33, caption 44); 17. Train ticket from Marseille to Orange, Vaucluse, France, March 1940. The Armoured Force Training Centre was based around Piolenc, 4 miles north of Orange with the 1st and 2nd Tank Battalions based at nearby St.Cecile-Les-Vignes.

For details of other military history titles published by Helion & Company Limited contact the above address, or visit our website: http://www.helion.co.uk.

We always welcome receiving book proposals from prospective authors.

Contents

Dedication and thanks ... iv

Foreword ... v

Map ... vi

Introduction ... vii

I   1939 ... 11

II   1940–44 ... 21

III   1944–45 ... 63

IV   1945–47 ... 129

Appendix: Order of Battle ... 143

Bibliography ... 145

Dedication

To my father Aleksander Leon 'Manka' Jarzembowski, a professional soldier of Poland, who served his country in seven campaigns between 1917–1945.

To my half-brother, Tadeusz 'Jarski' Jarzembowski, founder of Solidarity with Solidarity (1981).

Father and son, both patriots, doing their duty for the restoration of Poland's freedom.

Thanks

My gratitude goes to David Bradley whose knowledge and unstinting enthusiasm were hugely appreciated.

I would like to thank the following who offered invaluable advice and support, Evan McGilvray, Ken Tout, Tony Colvin, David Paintin, Kuba and Kazik Jarzembowski, Richard Szczawinski, Jacques Van-Dijke, Dr. Jens Graul, Neale Parsons and Zygmunt Kopel.

My special thanks goes to my son Nick, who has constructed a website dedicated to the 1st Polish Armoured Division (www.armouredhussars.com).

Foreword

This wonderful album is a brilliant pictorial history of the 1st Polish Armoured Division composed of about 250 photographs, documents and publications largely collected by WO1 Alexsander Leon 'Manka Jarzembowski', a veteran of 2nd Armoured Regiment, as he soldiered for Poland between 1917–1949.

The collection lay in albums unseen for decades until recent interest in the Division and its Commanding Officer, General Stanislaw Maczek caused Jarzembowski's son, Jan, to revisit his father's archive in order to provide a narrative for the almost forgotten Division and for his father's memory.

The photographs themselves cover the period from 1939 and the invasion of Poland before moving onto the French Campaign of 1940; the bulk of the images lie with the story of the Division from arriving in the UK in 1940, reforming in 1942 and then from 1944 including its pursuit of the Germans across Northern France, Belgium and Holland and finally into Germany. Included are some of the final Divisional parades prior to disbandment in 1947. There are also many interesting photographs of dignitaries who visited and inspected the Division thorough out those years, including General Sikorski – see Monty's incredible furry gauntlets for example!

The range of images available in this album is wide and impressive with many excellent shots of uniforms, equipment and armour. Not only does it provide an aid to historians and veterans' families, but it will be of great value to military modellers, too.

This album is a tribute to the gallant men of the Polish 1st Armoured Division and it is to this end that I am proud to dedicate this foreword to the memory of General Maczek and his men, who so bravely fought the Second World War from the very beginning to the very end but gained nothing for their efforts. They maintained their dignity and pride to the end of their, often, very long lives.

Evan McGilvary
29 January 2013

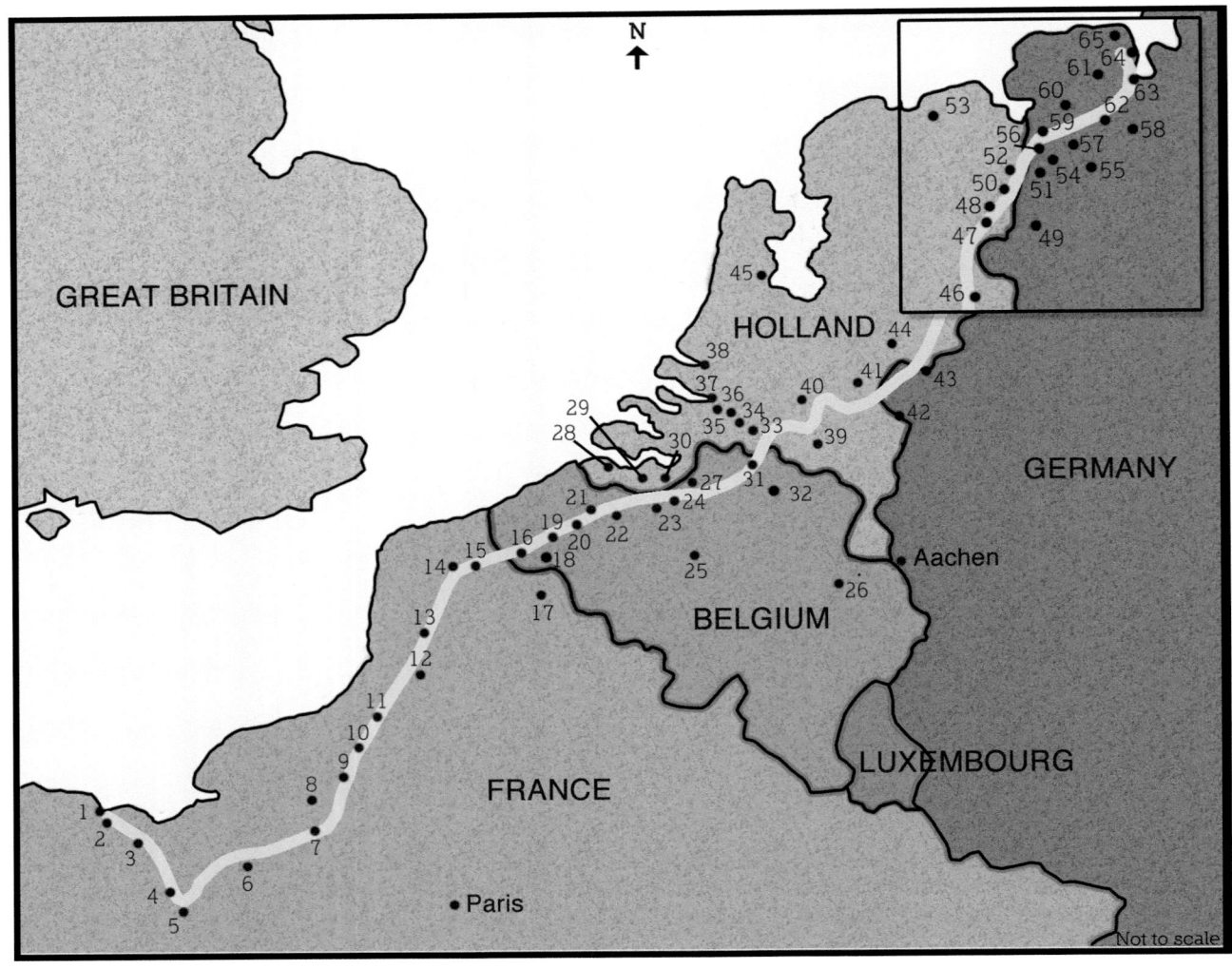

Main operational route of the 1st Polish Armoured Division 1944–45

1. Arromanches-Les-Bains
2. Bayeux
3. Caen
4. Falaise
5. Chambois
6. Bernay
7. Elbeuf
8. Rouen
9. Buchy
10. Neufchatel-en-Bray
11. Blangy-sur-Bresle
12. Abbeville
13. Hesdin
14. St.Omer
15. Blaringhem
16. Poperinge
17. Lille
18. Ypres
19. Roulers
20. Thielt
21. Ruiselede
22. Ghent
23. St.Niklaas
24. Beveren-Waas
25. Brussels
26. Leige
27. Antwerp
28. Terneuzen
29. Axel
30. Hulst
31. Merksplas
32. Turnhout
33. Alphen
34. Breda
35. Terheijden
36. Zevenbergschen Hoek
37. Moerdijk
38. Rotterdam
39. Eindhoven
40. Hertogenbosch
41. Nijmegen
42. Goch
43. Rees
44. Arnhem
45. Amsterdam
46. Goor
47. Hengelo
48. Coevorden
49. Meppen
50. Ter Apel
51. Oberlangen
52. Bourtange
53. Groningen
54. Rhede
55. Papenburg
56. Stapelmoor Heide
57. Detern
58. Oldenburg
59. Leer
60. Hesel
61. Friedeburg
62. Westerstede
63. Varel
64. Wilhemshaven
65. Jever

Introduction – First to Fight

The dawn of tank warfare was witnessed by Polish soldiers in exile (known as "The Blue Army", after their French issued uniforms and later as 'Haller's Army", after their commander, Józef Haller) fighting alongside the French Army on the Western Front during the last years of World War I, as part of their struggle for an independent Poland. Shortly after the end of the war, in early 1919, the 1st Polish Tank Regiment was formed. Equipped with French Renault light tanks it was immediately transported to newly restored Poland to resist the threat of Soviet invasion. During the Polish-Soviet War (1919-1921) fledging armoured units, although small in number, were often decisive in small local engagements. The inter-war years saw the further development of the Armoured Forces, with armour becoming a separate branch of the Polish Army.

On the eve of war in 1939 the Polish Armoured forces comprised three light tank battalions, largely equipped with 95 Polish 7TP tanks, 35 previously purchased British Vickers tanks, some recently delivered French R35s and 55 Renault FT-17s, some of which had seen service against the Bolsheviks. In addition several hundred lightly armoured TK/TKS tankettes were deployed amongst the infantry divisions and cavalry brigades supported by some 10 armoured trains.

At 04:48 on 1 September 1939 the German Battleship *Schleswig-Holstein* opened fire on the Polish garrison of Westerplatte on the outskirts of Danzig, thus beginning the Polish Campaign and unleashing World War II. Soon afterwards, code-named Operation WEISS, the German forces crossed the border with Army Group North driving south from Pomerania and East Prussia with the main assault by Army Group South launched from Silesia, tasked with enveloping the Polish forces along the Western frontier and then onto Warsaw. The Poles were outnumbered in all aspects with their 26 divisions and 12 brigades facing an assortment of 50 German divisions including six Panzer, across two army groups.

The Poles had two motorised armoured formations (with plans for more to follow), the 10th Cavalry Brigade and the Warsaw Armoured Brigade. The 10th Cavalry Brigade was commanded by Colonel Stanisław Maczek (later commander of 1st Polish Armoured Division) and was the reserve unit of Army Krakow. The Brigade engaged the Germans around Krakow, taking advantage of the mountainous and hilly terrain and managed to hold off German attacks, before falling back into Hungary, where it was interned. Many of the veterans, including Maczek, now made their way to France.

The Warsaw Armoured Brigade was commanded by Colonel Stefan Rowecki. At the outbreak of war, the Brigade was rushed into service although not fully operational. Largely equipped with tankettes and British made Vickers light tanks, it was seconded to Army Lublin. Following various engagements their final battle was on 16 September, around the town of Tomaszow Lubelski. The unit suffered heavy losses and was shortly afterwards disbanded on 20 September with those remaining crossing into Hungary. However Rowecki stayed in Poland and in 1942 he became the commander of the main Polish resistance movement, Armia Krajowa (AK-Home Army) until he was arrested in June 1943. In August 1944, he was executed by the Germans.

The Poles' main plan was to deploy their forces close to the Western border, forward of major rivers to shield their mobilization and to allow for an eventual withdraw eastwards avoiding major battles. This strategy of defensive manoeuvre had been used against the Russians in the Polish-Soviet war but the Poles completely underestimated the speed and power of the German mechanized assault supported by air superiority. Also even with the announcement of the Molotv-Ribbontrop Pact, the Soviet-German non-aggression agreement signed on 23 August, Poland's eastern frontiers were left largely unguarded, as the threat was still perceived as coming from the West.

Allied support from Great Britain and France was severely miscalculated and had minimal impact on the campaign. By May 1939 both countries had pledged support for Poland. On 7 September the French launched a half-hearted attack into the Rhine area, known as the Saar Offensive. The French advanced, five miles, largely unopposed into German territory before a withdrawal was ordered to the Maginot Line, due to the implementation of their defensive strategy. Furthermore the Allies had pressured Poland into initially restricting full mobilisation due to the misplaced view that it would speed the onset of war as experienced during the First World War. This resulted in the mobilisation of only two-thirds of Poland's forces by the time Germany attacked.

The Polish military leadership, under Marshall Edward Rydz-Śmigły, had not reckoned on the pace of the German attacks and deployed their forces to block the drive on Warsaw. Despite some local Polish successes, the Germans continued their advance on Warsaw and a gap developed between the Polish armies. The order was given to fall back over the Vistula. A counter attack was launched on the Burza which put the German assault on Warsaw on hold. However the Polish counter-attack was unsustainable and the Germans seized the opportunity to encircle the Polish formations resulting in the destruction of two Polish armies. The German attack on Warsaw resumed and by 13 September the city was surrounded and surrendered on 27 September.

On 17 September the Red Army started its invasion of Eastern Poland. German forces had not been alerted to the Soviet action and over the next few days adjusted their positions to match the boundary lines agreed by the pre-war Molotv-Ribbontrop Pact. Everywhere the Polish military situation was disintegrating. The Polish High Command now ordered all surviving units to retreat into Romania with the aim of preserving as much of the Polish Army as possible. There was no national capitulation with Polish elements fighting on until the last battle on 6 October, at Kock, 88 miles south-east of Warsaw.

Overall the Polish armoured forces, deployed as infantry support, acquitted themselves well during the campaign and were able to score a number of significant, although local, successes. Of the 2,500 German tanks deployed, some 674 were knocked out during the campaign (217 were total write-offs). Although a majority of these losses were due to Polish anti-tank guns, a significant number had been put out of action by Polish armoured vehicles and their crews.

As the world observed the fast moving campaign in Poland, the name 'Blitzkrieg' was coined by America's *Time Magazine*, in an article on 28 September. This journalistic shorthand was to describe what many saw as the revolutionary use of fast moving powerful armoured formations, closely supported by aircraft, to achieve rapid victory.

The rallying call was to France and the formation of a new Polish Army. Some 35,000 troops reached France (some escapees made their way to Syria forming the nucleus of the Polish 2nd Corps). Camps were established in Western France with Coetquidan in Brittany as the main base, set-up on 12 September. There was initial optimism that as well as four infantry divisions a large armoured force could be created. However due to supply and time limitations the creation of a Polish Light Armoured Division was agreed, to be commanded by Maczek, recently appointed to Brigadier-General by General Władysław Sikorski, Commander-in-Chief of Polish Armed Forces in France. Progress was slow and resources, particularly vehicles, limited.

On 10 May, after the many months of "The Phoney War" (October 1939 to April 1940) on the Western Front, German forces invaded Holland and Belgium, as part of Operation GELB. In accordance with their advance planning, French Armies and the British Expeditionary Force (BEF) advanced into Belgium. However this was a feint as the main German attack was moving undetected through the densely forested Ardennes area. On 13 May the German Panzer divisions forced the Meuse at Sedan and along with other bridgeheads, broke out and raced westwards. Despite Allied resistance, the Panzers quickly reached the English Channel trapping the Allied armies fighting north of their line of advance. The BEF were able to consolidate their defenses, especially around the Dunkirk perimeter and with the fortuitous panzer halt order issued by Hitler, were able to evacuate 330,000 British and Allied soldiers (Operation DYNAMO 27 May to 4 June) although with the loss of all their vehicles and heavy weapons. The Polish Forces in France initially played no part in these battles.

On 5 June the Germans commenced Operation ROT, with the aim of destroying the remaining French armies. The initial German assaults across the Somme and Aisne faced heavy resistance, but by mid-June the Germans had made headway.

Maczek realized that an operational division was now impossible to achieve, so only a brigade-sized force was feasible. The 10th Cavalry Brigade was created, consisting of one tank regiment with two armoured battalions (the 1st equipped with the Renault 35 and the 2nd with the Renault 40), a motorised cavalry regiment of two battalions and various supporting units. Forced to deploy by the French the Brigade's first encounter was at Champaubert on 12 June. Although enjoying some success the Poles were constantly harassed by enemy armour and aircraft. Various engagements followed but resulted in a withdrawal towards Loire as the French armies collapsed. Due to chronic shortages of both fuel and ammunition, most of the vehicles and equipment were destroyed on 17/18 June. The survivors dispersed into smaller groups, ordered to make their way to unoccupied coastal areas of which about 19,000 were evacuated to Great Britain. An armistice was agreed on 22 June. Mazcek reached Britain via Marseilles, Algeria, Morocco and Lisbon onto London. For a second time in a year, work on establishing a Polish Army-in-exile began.

The Poles were based in Scotland and in October 1940 the Polish 1st Corps was established, using the surviving elements evacuated from France. In the same month the 1st Tank Regiment was formed and was expanded to form the 16th Tank Brigade in September 1941. Due to a lack of active Polish formations, General Sikorski, recently appointed Commander-in-Chief, in late 1940, ordered the formation of 12 crews (spread over four groups) for armoured trains to support British patrolling of coastal areas against a threat of German invasion. Manned largely by a surplus of officers, each train had a crew of 55 men. At the beginning of 1942 changes included the use of attached armoured vehicles, including Valentines, which enabled troops to be trained on armour mobility and maintenance. Each armoured train had a leased civilian engine and driver, two supply wagons, plus another two fitted out as fighting platforms, mounting a rotating 57mm Hotchkiss gun and machine guns. Due to steel shortages these wagons were reinenforced with concrete walls. With the threat of invasion over, the trains were finally disbanded by mid-1943. On 26 February 1942, the 1st Polish Armoured Division was formed, commanded by General Maczek, consisting of 10th Armoured Cavalry Brigade, 16th Armoured Brigade and various other divisional support units including Reconnaissance, Signals, Engineers and Transport.

During 1943, following the new British pattern, when one armoured brigade became the standard in an armoured division, the 1st Polish Armoured Division's armoured brigade was designated as the 10th Armoured Cavalry Brigade. Following

INTRODUCTION – FIRST TO FIGHT

extensive training the Division was mobilized on 19 March 1944 and embarked for France at the end of July. In Normandy the Poles joined General Montgomery's 21st Army Group, which consisted of 1st Canadian Army, British 2nd Army and a number of other foreign national contingents. Divisional strength would peak at around 16,000 men equipped with 381 tanks, 460 guns and 4000 vehicles.

The Division landed in France between 29 July and 4 August, moving to its assembly area around Bayeux. It then took up position on the start line for the forthcoming offensive, south of Caen on the eastern side of the main highway to Falaise.

The Division's first major action was as part of the Canadian Operation TOTALIZE which was launched south of Caen on 7 August with the Poles attacking on the left flank on 8 August. By 10 August the offensive had stalled in the face of heavy German resistance. A few days later another offensive, Operation TRACTABLE, made progress towards Falaise. The Canadians continued their attacks with the aim of linking up with US forces advancing from the south, following the failed German offensive at Mortain, and trapping the enemy in the Falaise area. On 16 August Polish armour and infantry occupied the summit of Mount Ormel, dominating the surrounding countryside and controlling the German escape routes from the Falaise pocket. Because of its shape this position was nicknamed Maczuga (Mace). The Poles found themselves attacked, both by enemy forces trying to escape from the trap, and elements of the 2nd SS Panzer Division, outside the encirclement, trying to force an escape route through the Polish defenders. In desperate fighting the Polish infantrymen and tank crews were able to resist all these assaults. This was a major feat of arms by the Poles. On the evening of 19 August Polish and American soldiers met at Chambois, sealing the pocket.

Following their defeat in Normandy, surviving German forces fled towards the German border with the Allies in hot pursuit across France and into Belgium.

The port of Antwerp had been captured by the British 11th Armoured Division on 4 September, largely intact. Unfortunately the Germans still held the approaches to the port along the River Scheldt which prevented its use to relieve the severe logistic problems the Allied armies were experiencing. Therefore both banks had to be cleared. To break German resistance on the north bank of the Scheldt it was decided that it was going to be necessary to clear the area south of the River Maas of enemy forces and the Division was one of the units assigned to British I Corps (part of 1st Canadian Army) to conduct this operation. By mid-September the Division attacked in the direction of the port of Terneuzen, capturing it on 20 September. Regrouping into defensive positions it was tasked to take Breda, with its ultimate objective to drive to the Maas and capture the bridges at Moerdijk. Resistance was stiff and the countryside favoured the defense. Both weather and terrain hampered the Polish attack with a battlefield riven by canals and dykes. On 29 October the Poles captured Breda.

The Division pushed on towards the line of the River Mark – Mark Canal. Every effort to establish bridgeheads over the Mark was furiously resisted by elements of the German 15th Army. It was not until 5 November that the Mark was crossed. Over the next three days the Division fought its way forward, only to find, on reaching the Maas, that the Moerdijk bridges had been destroyed.

The approach of winter brought major operations to a halt. However minor actions and patrolling (albeit deadly) kept the Division active. At about this time there was a major re-equipping of the Division. Like the other standard armoured divisions in 21st Army Group (Guards Armoured, 7th Armoured, 11th Armoured and 4th Canadian) the Poles had been equipped with Sherman Mk Vs and Sherman Fireflies with their 17 pdr guns. Many of these types in the 1st Polish Armoured Division were now replaced by Sherman Mk IIAs with 76mm guns, the only 21st Army Group armoured formation to be so re-equipped.

Although not involved in repelling the German offensive in the Ardennes, the Poles were involved in heavy fighting in December. As a result of Canadian concerns, the Division attacked the Fallschirmjäger garrison at Kapelsche Veer on the southern bank of the Maas but without success. It was not until January that the Canadians took the position.

On 14 April 1945 the Division stood on the Dutch-German border for its final offensive of the war, reaching the River Ems near the German border on 18 April.

By 19 April the Division had completed its task of clearing north-east Holland and was advancing towards north-west Germany, along the line Neuenberg – Wittmund – Jever. Following the surrender, to Field Marshall Montgomery, of all German Forces in North-West Germany, Denmark and the Netherlands on 4 May, with the ceasefire declared for 08.00 hours on 5 May, Lieutenant-General Simonds (Canadian 2nd Corps) gave the Poles the honour of accepting the German surrender of the port and garrison of Wilhelmshaven. This was duly carried out both efficiently and without incident. The Division went on to form part of the British occupation forces in Germany (British Army of the Rhine, previously the 21st Army Group) until being disbanded in 1947.

As a consequence of the coming to power of a Communist regime in Poland, many veterans of the Division decided not to return home. Many established new lives abroad, especially in Great Britain, where the Polish Resettlement Corp (PRC) was established until final demobilisation and disbanding in 1949. The collapse of Communism in Eastern Europe (1989) finally enabled the survivors of the 1st Polish Armoured Division to receive due recognition of their exploits from their homeland and to return home.

Part I

1939

1. Lublin, Poland, 24 April 1932. Personnel of a Motor Transport Company (formed the cadre of the 9th Armoured Battalion, based in the district of Bronowice, Lublin in 1935) with A.L.Jarzembowski kneeling second row, third from right. In 1933 the Motor Transport Battalions were merged with the armoured forces. These armoured forces had initially been conceived by the formation of the 1st Tank Regiment in 1919, equipped with Renault M1917 FT tanks, fighting in the Polish-Soviet War (1919–1921). Extended to three battalions, the unit became a separate branch of the Polish Army in 1930. Renamed the 1st Armoured Regiment in 1931, various changes of organisation followed resulting in 1937 with the formation of three Groups supported by two other armoured units, the 10th Cavalry Brigade and the Warsaw Motorised Brigade.

2. Poland, 1938. Presentation ceremony of the standard of the 2nd Armoured Regiment, 10th Cavalry Brigade. The Brigade was fully mechanized with around 3000 troops and commanded by Colonel Stanisław Maczek, from October 1938. In that year the uniform was changed for officers and non-commissioned officers (NCO) to all black leather jackets, larger black berets and the German 1916 steel helmet. This appearance gained them the nicknames 'The Black Brigade' by the Poles and 'Black Devils' by the Germans. The Brigade was later commemorated by the issue of a black left shoulder strap, worn on the British army issued uniform. The tank shown is one of 38 Vickers 6-ton tanks imported from the United Kingdom in 1931. Also shown are two Polish Fiat 508/IIIs, a Lazik all-terrain, door-less, four passenger car, often used in the reconnaissance role.

3. Poland, September 1939. A Panzerkampfwagen (Pz.Kpfw) III Ausf. E mounting a 37mm gun passes a Sonderkraftfahrzeug (Sd.Kfz) 221 or 222 light armoured car. Although the mainstay of the Panzer divisions later in the war, only 98 of this type were in service in the September Campaign, with a dozen in each panzer division. The tank is displaying a plain white Balkan cross, the standard German army insignia in 1939. It was replaced after the Polish campaign by the more familiar, and less conspicuous, black cross with white outline, as operational experience had shown that the original insignia had provided a perfect aiming point for Polish anti-tank gunners.

4. Poland, September 1939. A knocked-out Pz.Kpfw II amid ruins of a Polish town. This tank was designed to be more heavily armed than its predecessor the Pz.Kpw I and was armed with a 20mm Kampfwagenkanone (tank gun) as well as a machine gun. Some of the crews in-filled the centre of the Balkan crosses with yellow paint to prevent its use as a target marker, as in this example, or applied dirt to tone it down.

5. Poland, 6 September 1939. A large concentration of German lorries and other support vehicles near Krakow. In the centre foreground Krupp 'Protze' (limber) personnel carriers are seen which were also used as light artillery limbers. Two of the formations attacking Krakow, defended, amongst others, by the Polish 10th Mechanised Brigade, were the 2nd Panzer and 3rd Gebirgsjäger (Mountain) divisions. As the latter was configured for operations in mountainous areas and was therefore accordingly equipped on a light scale, this mass of vehicles probably forms a major part of the logistic trains of the 2nd Panzer Division.

6. Poland, September 1939. A knocked-out or abandoned Polish 7TP (*dwuwiezowy*–twin turret) tank. Adapted from a British Vickers design and licensed built in Poland, 40 were fitted with two turrets mounting machine guns. This one has had one of its turret machine guns removed. A further 95 were equipped with a single turret mounting a Bofors 37mm gun.

7. Poland, September 1939. An abandoned Polish TK/TKS tankette. Like a number of other militaries during the inter-war period, the Poles were impressed by the potential of tankettes. In September 1939 the Polish army deployed some 450 TK/TKS of which 40 were equipped with a potent 20mm anti-tank gun. Note, the right side track is missing and its 7.92mm machine gun has been removed

8. Poland, October 1939. *Ciagnik Gasienicowy C2P* (Caterpillar tractor). At least five tractors can be seen in this vehicle collection point. The tractor was built on the chassis of the TK tankette and had a tarpaulin which could be removed as shown and was used in a variety of roles including towing trailers and artillery pieces. This version was part of a anti-aircraft battery, its Bofors (wz.36) 40mm anti-aircraft gun can be seen immediately behind, minus its wheels. At the top centre, there is a large building, possibly a bunker with a group of German soldiers standing in front of it.

9. Poland, September 1939. An abandoned Polish 7TP (*jednowiezowy*-single turret) light tank, belonging to either the 2nd or 3rd Light Tank Battalion. This version armed with a Bofors 37mm gun and fitted with a diesel engine, was superior to most German armour encountered during the campaign. Its biggest deficiency was its lack of numbers, with some 95 operational (compared to 98 PzKw III and 211 PzKw IV).

10. Polish/Hungarian border 1939. On 19 September 1,500 survivors (from the original 3,000) of the 10th Cavalry Brigade, together with their remaining equipment, crossed the border into Hungary to be interned. Many of the former members of the Brigade made their way first to France, and later to the United Kingdom, to continue the fight against the Germans. Their vehicles and equipment remained in Hungary. Here two Hungarian gendarmes guard an interned TK/TKS tankette, with Polish soldiers in the background. The majority of TK/TKS tankettes mounted a single 7.92mm machine-gun. (Wiatrowski, Tadeusz, *2nd Polish Armoured Regiment in Action, From Caen to Wilhelmshaven*. Schlutersche Buchdruckerei, Hannover, 1946)

11. France, 20 February 1940. A disembarkation card issued in Marseilles, stating that NCO Alexsander Jarzembowski arrived on the steamer *Varsovie* on 20 February 1940 and is lodged in barrack 9–3 and has been given the enrolment number 9305, having sailed from Greece.

12. Camp de Bressuire, France, February 1940. Polish soldiers, some of whom are dressed in their newly-issued French uniforms, with Polish insignia on their forage caps, pose for a photo. A.L.Jarzembowski, NCO, 1st Battalion Chars de Combat (1st Tank Battalion) is in civilian clothes, third from left.

13. Sainte Cecile-les-Vignes, France, 27 March 1940. Certificate belonging to A.L. Jarzembowski serving as an NCO in the Polish Army in France from 20 February 1940; stationed at Camp de Carpiagne until 25 February 1940; Camp de Bressuire, 26 February 1940 to 21 March 1940; Camp de Parthenay, 22 March 1940 to 26 March 1940; and from 27 March in 1st Tank Battalion, Sainte Cecile-les-Vignes. Signed by the Commanding Officer L. Zyrkiewicz, on 27 March 1940.

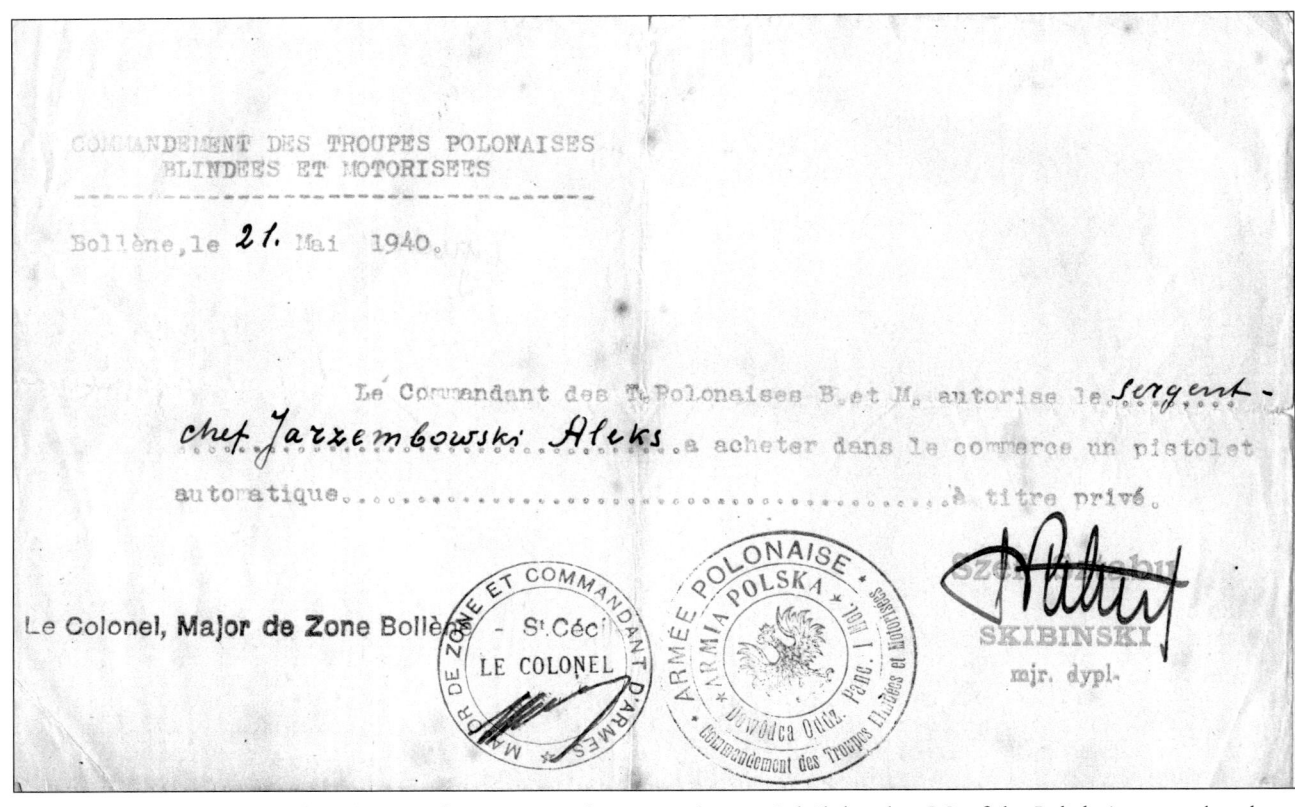

14. France, 21 May 1940. This certificate is an authorisation by Lt. Col Skibinski, CO of the Polish Armoured and Motorised Troops, permitting Sergeant A.L. Jarzembowski to buy an automatic pistol for his own private use.

15. France 1940. Renault R-35, a light tank introduced into the French Army in 1937, and designed to equip tank battalions that would act in the infantry support role. Although relatively well-armoured, it was slow and its short 37mm gun proved an inadequate anti-tank weapon. Prior to the outbreak of war, the Poles, had ordered a consignment of around 50 R-35 tanks, having previously been refused the superior Souma S35. Most equipped 21st Light Tank Battalion, used to defend the "Romania Bridgehead". Surviving vehicles withdrew into Romania where they were taken over by the Romanian Army. Note the French Armoured white hand-grenade marking, centre side panel.

16. France, June 1940. The 10th Armoured Cavalry Brigade consisted of a tank regiment with 1st and 2nd Tank Battalions. The former is seen here with the Renault R-35 infantry tank with the latter issued the Renault R-40. However due to the threatened collapse of the French front following the German attack on 5 June, the Brigade was rushed into battle not fully operational. The Brigade's unofficial marking was a poppy, derived from the translation of its commander's name, Maczek. (Wiatrowski, Tadeusz, *2nd Polish Armoured Regiment in Action, From Caen to Wilhelmshaven*. Schlutersche Buchdruckerei, Hannover, 1946)

17. The Polish Liner *Sobieski* was used as a troopship during Operation Ariel (or Aerial) 15 to 25 June 1940, the code name given to the evacuation of Allied forces in Western France (the formal end of hostilities between France and Germany being declared for the 25 June). Operating around the Ports of Bayonne and St. Jean-de-Luz, near the Spanish border, instructions had been issued that troops should make their way to the coast for embarkation, however those unable to embark were to travel overland through Spain to Portugal and then embark for England. Sergeant-Major A. L. Jarzembowski (centre) stands on the deck, having boarded at Bayonne on the 23 June, destination Plymouth. Troops were then transferred to Haydock Park Racecourse (Merseyside) and then onto three military camps in Scotland.

Part II

1940–44

18. Crawford Camp, South Lanarkshire, Scotland 1940. Polish soldiers, newly arrived from the continent and dressed in their French uniforms, admire a welcoming group of Scottish pipers from the Cameronians (Scottish Rifles). On 25 June 1940 orders were issued for the formation of a Polish armoured unit with Crawford becoming the Polish Armoured Forces Centre. This was followed with the creation of the Polish 1st Corps in October 1940 based at Perth.

19. Stonyburn, West Lothian, Scotland 9 August 1940. Polish soldiers wearing a combination of French and British uniforms reflect on home with Sergeant Major A.L.Jarzembowski, extreme right. Note a member of the 10th Cavalry Brigade, dressed in his black leather coat, left background.

20. **Motorised armoured drill instruction booklet, Great Britain, 1941.** (Musztra Pancerno Motorowa). Issued by the Supreme Commander and Minister of Military Affairs, Central Regulations Committee. Light grey cover (18cm × 12cm).

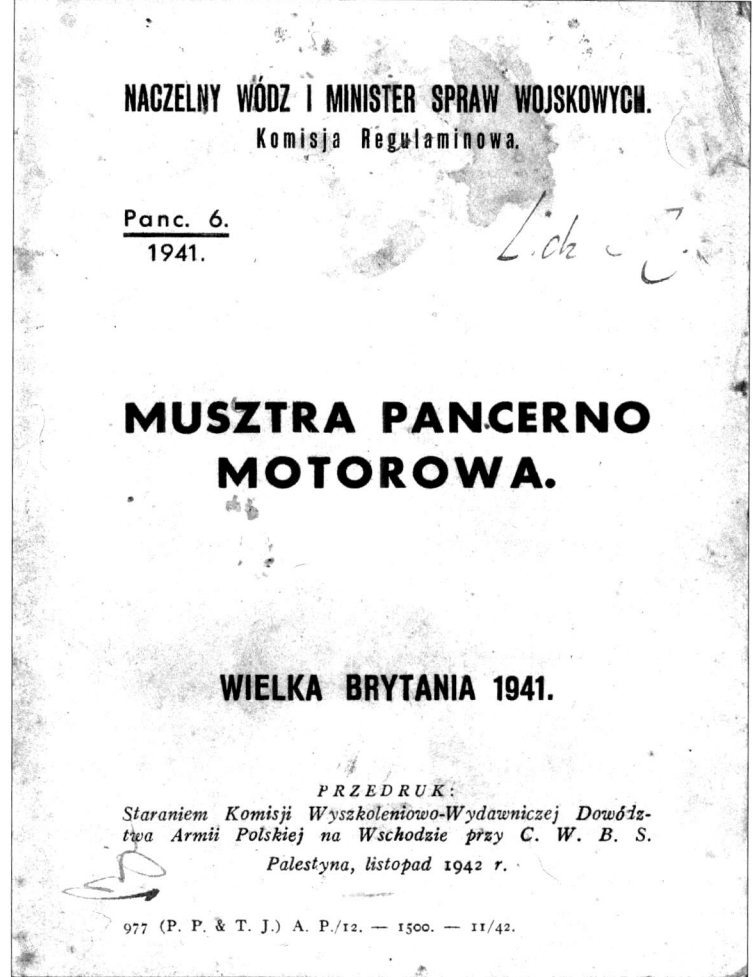

L. p.	Znaczenie znaków.	Znak ręką.		Dźwiękiem (gwizdek).	Światłem latarki.*)
		Sposób podawania.	Rys.		
1	„Uwaga". „Baczność". „Gotów". „Zrozumiano".	Ręka (dłonią zwróconą do odbiorcy) podniesiona pionowo do góry.		Jeden długi gwizd. / —— /	Jeden długi błysk.. / —— /
2	„Omyłka". „Nie rozumiem". „Niema przejścia".	Ruchy przeczące prawą (lewą) ręką jak przy ścieraniu tablicy.		Po dwa krótkie gwizdki z przerwami. / .. / .. /	Po dwa krótkie błyski nadawane z przerwami. / .. / .. /
3	„Przy wozach zbiórka".	Prawe przedramie zgięte poziomo nad głową.		Jeden długi jeden krótki gwizd. / —— . /	Jeden długi jeden krótki błysk. / —— . /
4	„Dcy wozów (a gdy podaje ten znak dca komp. znaczy dcy plutonów) zbiórka".	Prawe ramię w bok, przedramię pionowo, dłoń jak do salutowania.		Jeden długi dwa krótkie gwizdki. / —— .. /	Jeden długi dwa krótkie błyski. / —— .. /
5	„Zbiórka" (wszyscy do mnie).	Wyprostowanie ramion poziomo w bok i skrzyżowanie ich na piersiach frontem do odbiorcy znaku. (Ruchy zagarniające.)		Dwa długie i dwa krótkie gwizdki. / —— —— .. /	Dwa długie i dwa krótkie błyski. / —— —— .. /

Tablica I.
ZNAKI RĘKĄ (DŹWIĘKIEM, ŚWIATŁEM LATARKI).

*) Nie dotyczy to sygnalizacji świetlnej stałej zmontowanej na czołgu.

21. **Page from Motorised armoured drill instruction booklet.** Hand signals.

22. Scotland early 1942. Valentine tanks, received in November 1941 of 16th Tank Brigade, I Polish Corps, loaded onto flatcars. Crewmen wear their French issue uniforms and equipment, seen here wearing the 1935 pattern brown leather jacket, the old 1876/93 pattern pistol holster and goggles issued to motorised troops. The figure standing third from left, appears to be wearing the British Army motorcyclists' protective (rubberised) wet weather uniform as well as the long 1907 bayonet scabbard for the British Short Magazine Lee-Enfield rifle (SMLE).

23. Scotland early 1942. Another view of Valentines, seen in photo 22, on leased flat-cars from the London Midland and Scottish Railway (LMS).

PART II: 1940–44   25

24. Scotland early 1942. Infantry Tank Mk III, Valentine II, 65th Tank Battalion, 16th Tank Brigade, I Polish Corps. Tank crew and soldiers pose for the camera with the soldier on the right wearing a British pattern greatcoat and a despatch rider's rubberised cotton helmet. A rifle is seen immediately behind him. Note the Michelin man figure on the tank turret, a souvenir from France (the second soldier from the right can be seen in photo 22).

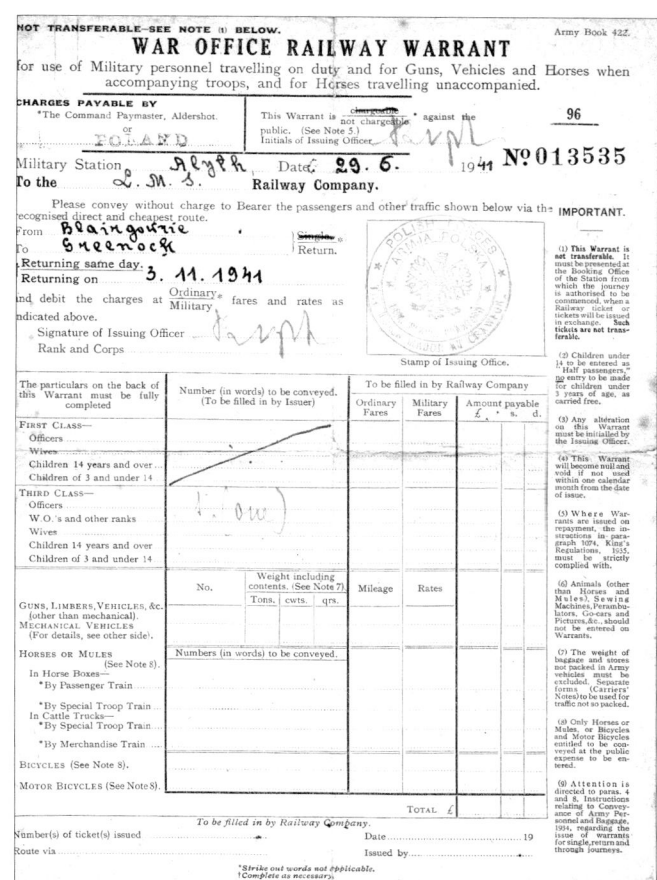

25. War Office Railway warrant no: 013535. (25cm × 18cm, manila colour with the Polish Forces stamp in red ink) granted to Staff Sergeant A.L. Jarzembowski, Polish Forces in Scotland, 29 June 1941, from the military station at Alyth, travelling from Blairgowrie to Greenock, return. The warrant was used for military personnel travelling on duty and for guns, vehicles and horses when accompanying troops.

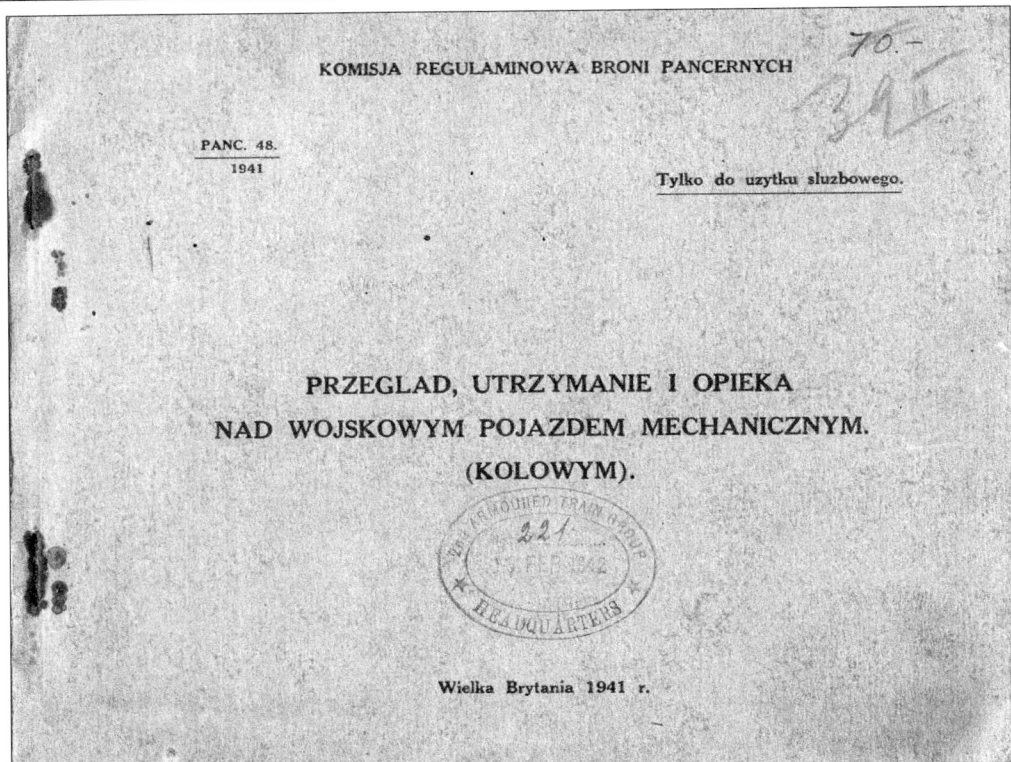

26. Instruction Manual, Great Britain, 1941. Inspection, maintenance and care of a military motor vehicle, translated into Polish from the standard British Army issue booklet. Orange paperback booklet (16cm × 20.5cm). Note stamp of 2nd Armoured Train Group Headquarters, 16 February 1942.

27. Scotland early 1942. Infantry Tank Mk III, Valentine II of the 65th Tank Battalion, 16th Tank Brigade, I Polish Corps. Crews pose for the camera, note their French issue uniforms.

28. Scotland early 1942. Same group as in photo 27.

29. Scotland early 1942. Valentine crews being briefed. French leather jackets are in evidence, however the soldier on the right is in British battledress. The ranks are signified on their berets, one bar a Lance Corporal, two bars a Corporal, three bars a Lance Sergeant, a chevron a Sergeant, a star Second Lieutenant and two stars a Lieutenant. Observe also the Michelin man figure on the tank turret. Note that the rank insignia is worn to the left of the centrally positioned national eagle cap badge. This was changed in February 1943, when rank was worn under the eagle on all berets and forage caps.

30. Scotland late early 1942 (sequential photos 30–36). Infantry Tank Mk III, Valentine II, 66th Tank Battalion, 16th Tank Brigade, I Polish Corps. A column of Valentines on manoeuvres. The driver's position was on the centre-line of the tank allowing him to enter/exit the vehicle from either side and in this case both of the front hatches can be seen open. Note Michelin man figure on turret, seen in previous photos and also visible is the unique "T" number assigned to all British tanks, number T1290248.

31. Scotland early 1942. Infantry Tank Mk III, Valentine II, 66th Tank Battalion, 16th Tank Brigade, I Polish Corps. Close-up of a tank from photo (30). The crew are wearing French issue uniforms including the 1935 pattern motorised troops' helmet issued to all crews of any Armoured Fighting Vehicle (AFV). The markings are, left to right, PL (Poland), 16 (bridge classification tonnage number), 073 (66th Tank Battalion) and the circle/wing (I Polish Corps).

32. Scotland early 1942. Infantry Tank Mk III, Valentine II, shown is the driver's position of a Valentine seen from the front of the vehicle. The driver's visor is open. To navigate under "closed down" conditions in combat the visor would be closed and the driver would navigate using the two periscopes mounted above and to the right and left of the visor. Note the driver is wearing goggles which would be a useful protection against dust and debris generated by his own vehicle's movements as well as that caused by any vehicles ahead. Note camouflage marking.

33. Scotland early 1942. Infantry Tank Mk III, Valentine II. The driver's compartment seen through the left-hand hatch. The right hand hatch is also open. One of the driver's periscopes is prominent on the left hand side of the photo. The driver is wearing a beret and protective goggles and his French tank crewman helmet is readily to hand at his right side.

34. Scotland early 1942. Infantry Tank Mk III, Valentine II. A tank commander, a Lance Sergeant (three bars on his beret) in the turret of his Valentine Mk II, illustrating the cramped conditions inside the vehicle. He is using the radio either to communicate to his crew or to other vehicles on his unit's radio "net". The compact nature of the Valentine II limited its crew to three. The later Valentine Mk III, with a re-designed larger turret, allowed an additional crewman. However when later versions were up-gunned with 6 pounders, the crew complement reverted to three to make way for the larger weapon.

35. Scotland early 1942. Valentine tanks, 66th Tank Battalion, 16th Tank Brigade, I Polish Corps.

36. Scotland early 1942. Valentine tanks, the 3 man-crew. Jerzy Niewinowski is seen crouching by the tank tracks on the extreme left. They appear to have the French issued, Spanish manufactured, 'Ruby' pistol.

37. Scotland early 1942. A Lance Sergeant stands by a 3 Ton 4x2 GS Ford 01T V8, probably Canadian-built.

POLAND

Army Form A. 2038.

Identification Card for Mechanical Transport Drivers.

THE WAR OFFICE.

The undersigned 3239 staff/sgt Aleksander Jarzembowski
(description) 1st. Tanks Regiment.

being employed on Military Service, is hereby authorized by the Secretary of State for War to drive a motor car, lorry, motor cycle or other mechanically propelled vehicle when on Government duty.

Signature of Holder staff sgt mjr   Permanent Under-Secretary of State for War.

Available from 1 May 1941 to 30 Apr. 1942.

(16531) Wt.33875/1199 500,000 12/40 A.& E.W.Ltd. **Gp.698** Forms/A.2038/5.

38. Identification Card for Mechanical Transport Drivers, issued by the War Office (7.5cm × 10cm manila card with POLAND in red ink) valid May 1941 to April 1942. Issued to Staff Sergeant A.L. Jarzembowski, 1st Tank Regiment, counter-signed on the reverse by Major Obloczynski.

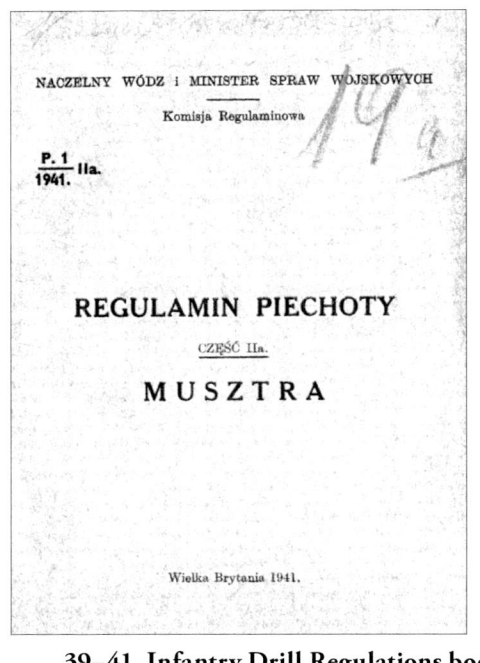

39–41. Infantry Drill Regulations booklet, Great Britain, 1941, light blue paperback cover, (17cm × 12.5 cm) illustrated throughout.

42. Commemorative card for the Polish 16th Tank Brigade (Smok – dragon), Kelso, Scotland, 28 October 1943. The Brigade was formed on 19 September 1941 and had three tank battalions, 65th, 66th and 67th and was organised on a British tank brigade structure. In mid-August 1942, it was renamed the 16th Armoured Brigade with the three battalions becoming armoured regiments.

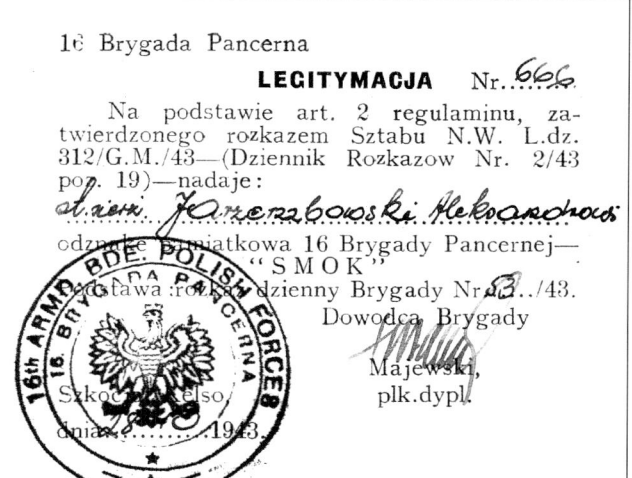

43. Commemorative card. Reverse side of card in photo 42, issued to A.L. Jarzembowski, signed by Colonel Tadeusz Majewski.

44. Scotland, Spring, 1942. A soldier wearing the badge of the 16th Tank Brigade, photographs a visit by General Anders.

45. Auberon Herbert (1922–1952) Scotland, 1942. Herbert with Staff Sergeant A.L. Jarzembowski and an unidentified Polish soldier. Auberon Herbert was the son of a Conservative member of Parliament and brother-in-law to Evelyn Waugh, the famous novelist. His expertise on Polish affairs enabled him to serve with the Polish Forces in Normandy, probably in a liaison role. Post war he supported several Eastern European anti-communist groups as well as supporting the resettlement of Polish exiles in the U.K.

46. Blairgowrie, Scotland, 1942. Fully equipped Polish soldiers of 1st Corps (circled wing displayed on the left windscreen panel) aboard Chevrolet YS 4103 lorries (note War Department serial numbers on bonnet, preceded with the letter 'L' for Lorry above 15cwt). The helmet stencilled Polish Army eagle badge was introduced in late 1940 and was applied using yellow gas detecting paint.

47. Blairgowrie, Scotland, 1942. Rear view of vehicle convoy from 66th Tank Battalion (073) seen in photo 46. Note vehicle mounted Bren-gun used in the anti-aircraft role.

48. Scotland 1942. Sappers of 1st Battalion using a Morris Commercial CS8 Mk I, a multi-purpose vehicle developed in 1934 for the British Army. (Richard Szczawinski)

49. Scotland 1942. A sentry in a vehicle park poses for the camera. His unit identification triangular collar insignia are the black-over-orange pennons of the Armoured Forces, general service. However to help differentiate the three armoured regiments, metal Arabic numerals, numbering one to three, were worn on the shoulder straps. During 1943 to further assist with unit identification, a different coloured strip was added to the triangular collar pennon, which was replaced with a 'swallow-tail' pennon officially approved from September 1944, see photo 86. The first truck from the left is a Bedford OYD 3 ton 4 × 2 GS, the next vehicle appears to be a later version of the Morris commercial D 6 × 4 6 seater staff car, followed by a Ford 01T 30 cwt 4 × 2 GS (Australian). Note that all the vehicles have the circled wing of the Polish 1st Corps marking on their left wheel-arch and top left windscreen, as well as the national marking PL (Poland).

50. 16th Tank Brigade, Blairgowrie, Scotland, spring 1942 (sequential photos 50–53) Valentines of 1 Corps awaiting a visit from General Sikorski. A limited number of Valentine tanks were issued to the Polish forces in November 1941. Sikorski had ordered the formation of a Polish Armoured Division in September 1941, with its core to be formed from 10th Armoured Cavalry Brigade and 16th Tank Brigade.

51. Inspection of the Tank Brigade, Blairgowrie, Scotland, spring 1942. General Władysław Sikorski (1881–1943) beginning his inspection together with officers of the Brigade. Sikorski had a long and distinguished military career, serving first in the Austrian Army during World War I and later in Piłsudski's Polish Legion. He commanded an army in the Polish-Soviet War (1919-1921), but following Piłsudski's coup in May 1926 held no further military appointments before the war. Following the defeat of Poland in 1939 and the fall of France in 1940, Sikorski established the Polish Government in exile in London, with the appointments of both Prime Minister and Commander in Chief. It was a tragedy for his country when Sikorski was killed on 4 July 1943, his aircraft crashing while taking off from the airfield at Gibraltar.

52. Inspection of the 16th Tank Brigade by General Sikorski, accompanied to his right by Colonel Tadeusz Majewski Regimental commander who was promoted commander of the 10th Armoured Cavalry Brigade from October 1943 until 16 January 1945, then appointed as Deputy Chief of Staff, followed by promotion to second in command of the Division from 24 October 1945 to 1 February 1946.

53. Blairgowrie, Scotland, spring 1942. General Sikorski attempts to climb into the turret of a Valentine for a test drive, which was photographed for propaganda purposes.

54. Blairgowrie, Scotland, 1942. General Sikorski with General Marian Kukiel (1885–1972) commanding Officer of the Polish 1st Corps, 1940–42 and the Polish Minister of War between 1942–49. Seen here talking to infantrymen, probably from the 16th Dragoon Battalion which was raised as the Brigade's integral motor battalion following British Army organisation and practice.

55. Blairgowrie, Scotland, 1942. General Sikorski talking to soldiers seen in photo (54). All the soldiers are wearing standard British-issue battledress and equipment and have the Polish national insignia, a yellow painted eagle, stencilled on their helmets.

56. Blairgowrie, Scotland, 1942 (sequential photos 56–61). King Peter II (1923–1970) of Yugoslavia (centre) visiting the Polish 1st Corps, escorted by General Sikorski and Władysław Raczkiewicz (1885–1947) President of the Republic of Poland, 1939–1947. Following the German invasion on 6 April 1941, Yugoslavia offered limited resistance and surrendered on 17 April. King Peter, Yugoslavia's last king, escaped through Greece, onto Egypt and finally arrived in the U.K. in June 1941, serving in the Royal Air Force (RAF) and eventually settling in America post-war.

57. King Peter confers with General Sikorski and President Raczkiewicz. The visit included a parade review, a battle re-enactment and a tour of the camp.

58. King Peter stands in front of a Churchill II, escorted by three aides, two of whom are in uniform, and is invited to climb aboard the Churchill. Note two escorting British officers, one extreme left and the other rear centre.

59. General Sikorski, King Peter and President Raczkiewicz stand on the front deck of a Churchill tank.

60. King Peter descends into the Churchill tank. Polish Valentines are lined-up in the background.

61. General Sikorski, standing in front of President Raczkiewicz, peers into the turret hatch after King Peter has descended into the Churchill tank. General Kukiel can be seen standing extreme left, talking to a British officer. Note the Churchill has recently been delivered to the Corps and apart from its British 'T' (tank) number, no unit or national marking have yet been applied.

62. Lanarkshire, Scotland, 1941. (sequential photos 62–65) Seen here is a banner displayed with the National slogan 'National War Weapons Week grin and spare it'. The campaign was launched by the Government to encourage citizens to save money for the war effort, through various schemes such as War Bonds and to prevent a 'run-on-the-bank' which would create a financial crisis, particularly with the threat of invasion. Local authorities would designate a particular week of the year, throughout the duration of the war, to raise funds by such measures as organising military parades, demonstrations and exhibitions. Immediately to the left are some pipers and drummers of the Gordon Highlanders. Polish infantrymen with their new British battledress uniforms, stand in the background to the right with Scottish soldiers (Cadet unit) to the left behind the stage.

63. Lanarkshire, Scotland, 1941. Close up of two pipers of the Gordon Highlanders. The Pipe Band was based at the Infantry Training Centre (I.T.C) at Hamilton Race Course.

The National War Weapons Week campaign originated in the First World War, when local communities would raise funds for specific military items, such as a tank.

64. Lanarkshire, Scotland, 1941. Polish infantryman of 1st Corps wearing standard British army battledress with 1937 webbing. The majority are carrying Lee Enfield SMLE (Short, Magazine, Lee Enfield) Mk III rifles. Note the fifth and sixth soldiers from the right are each holding the Thompson M1928 machine gun with the clip removed. All the soldiers have the Polish national insignia, a yellow painted eagle, on their helmet.

65. Lanarkshire, Scotland, 1941. Troops from photo 64, taken from the opposite end of the parade.

66–68. Scotland, 1942. A column of Infantry Tank Mk III, Valentine II tanks of the 66th (073) Tank Battalion, 16th Tank Brigade, I Polish Corps on rural manoeuvres.

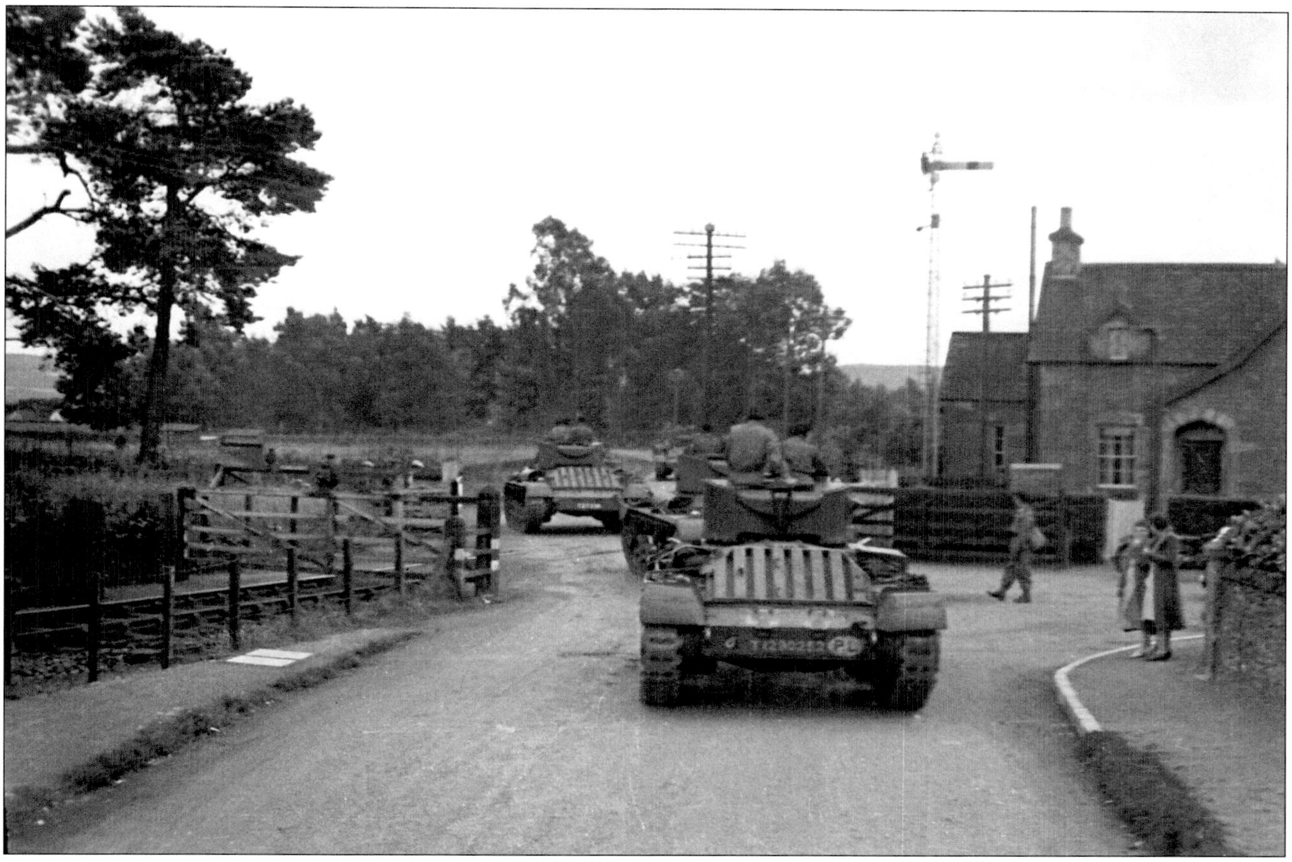

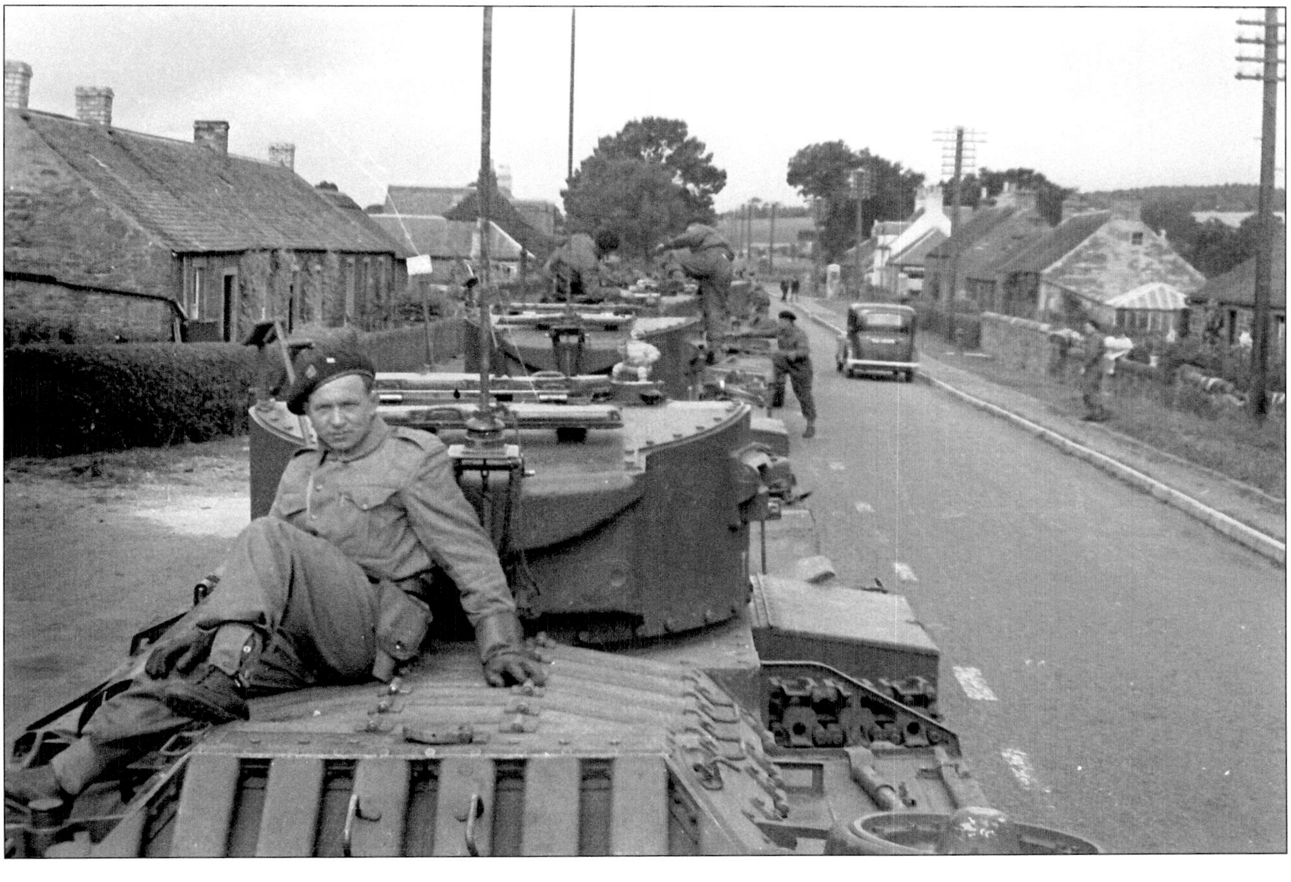

69–70. Scotland 1942. A column of Valentines (Infantry Tank Mk III, Valentine II) drawn up in a park for a local event, note fairground attractions in the background. This would enable members of the public to meet the Armed Forces and see their equipment first-hand, otherwise only seen in newspapers and cinema newsreels, and would certainly be a morale-booster for all participants.

71–72. Scotland 1941. A column of British Infantry Tank Mk IV Churchill IIs move along a road. Designed as an infantry support vehicle, some 15 tanks of this type were issued to the Poles in November 1941 and were assigned to the 65th Tank Battalion. They were unpopular with their Polish crews owing to their unreliability and demanding maintenance requirements.

73. Scotland early 1942. Churchill II's in a bivouac. Some Churchills have had their trackguards removed perhaps for maintenance purposes. None of the vehicles appear to display any obvious markings, apart from the British T (tank) production number. The Churchill II was armed with a 2pdr main armament, only served in the training role and did not see combat.

74. Scotland early 1942. Same Churchill tank bivouac as in photo 73. The crew appear to be conducting some basic maintenance. Note a crewman resting on the open left side hatch.

75. Scotland early 1942. The interior of a Churchill II. The driver's hatch is open. The Polish corporal is wearing battledress and his right hand seems to holding the firing mechanism of the hull-mounted machine gun, mounted on the left-hand side of the fighting compartment.

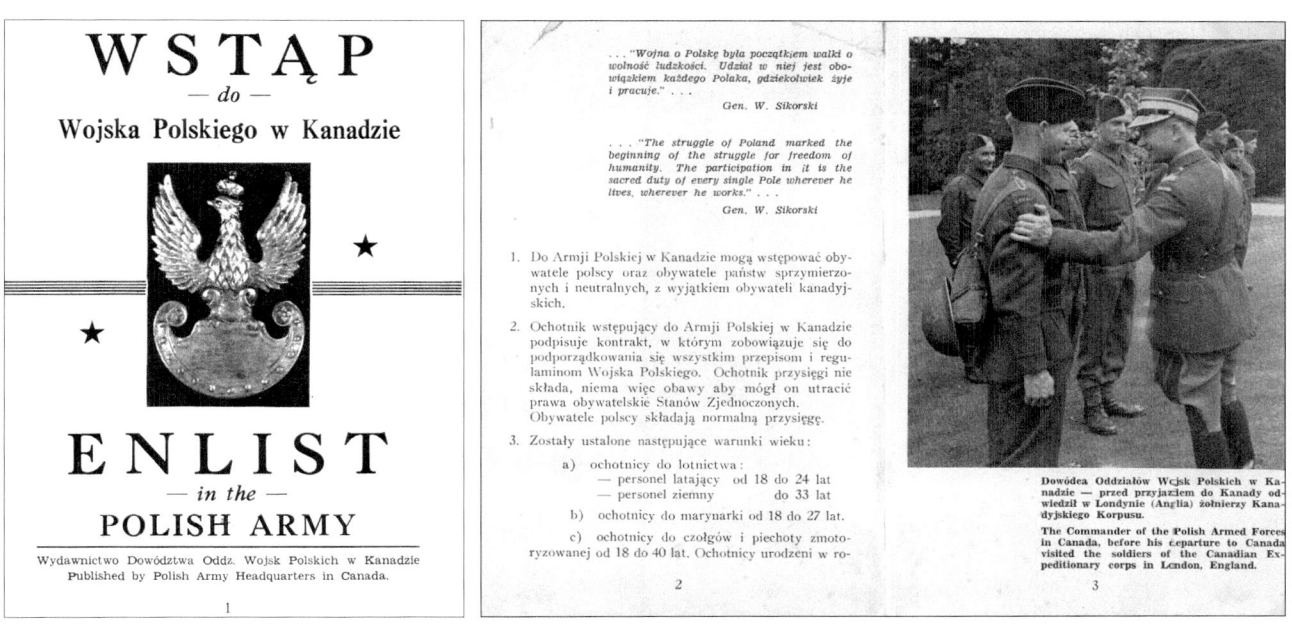

76–77. Join the Polish Army in Canada, pamphlet, circa 1942. Light grey (16cm × 11cm) with 11 pages, double-sided with information and photographs of the Polish Army in exile. General Sikorski made several visits to North America including Canada in April 1941 promoting enlistment. This resulted in the establishment of two Polish army training camps in Canada, with the proviso that any citizens of Allied and neutral countries could enlist with the exception of Canadian citizens. Furthermore it was illegal in America to allow enlistment in a foreign army. Due to both political and cultural reasons, the numbers of volunteers was hugely disappointing, with the majority preferring to join the American Forces.

78. General Władysław Anders (1892–1970) Commander of the Polish Army in the East visiting the 1st Polish Armoured Division. Scotland, April 1942. (sequential photos 78–80). During the First World War Anders, third from left salutes with General Klimecki, Chief of the General Staff (killed alongside General Sikorski in an air crash at Gibraltar, 4 July 1943) saw service with the Russian army. Joining the Polish Army he was a cavalry brigade commander at the outbreak of the Second World War. Withdrawing to the east he was taken prisoner by the Russians. Following the German invasion of Russia in June 1941, he was released and was appointed by General Sikorski to command a newly created Polish Army to fight alongside the Soviets. Due to political and supply issues, Anders and his men were evacuated to British Palestine where he formed the Polish 2nd Corps (1943–47), peaking at 103,000 troops. The Corps fought in the Italian campaign, attached to the British 8th Army, most notably at Monte Cassino in May 1944. Exiled in Britain, Anders became the Inspector General of the Polish Forces-in-Exile.

79. General Stanisław Maczek (1892–1994), Scotland, April 1942. Maczek can be seen wearing a traditional Rogatywka (garrison hat) standing fourth from Ander's right-side, next to General Klimecki. Maczek had a distinguished military career, spanning the First World War and the post-war struggles for Polish independence. He chose to live in exile in the United Kingdom until his country could be freed from Communism. Following the collapse of the regime in Poland, he was presented in 1994 with Poland's highest state decoration, the Order of the White Eagle. He is buried alongside those he commanded in the Polish military cemetery in Breda, Holland, the site of one of his Division's most impressive achievements.

80. General Władysław Anders, Scotland, April 1942. Anders bids his farewell to the Divisional Officers and is seen shaking hands with Colonel Tadeusz Majewski, observed by General Klimecki (centre).

81. Gosford House, near Longniddry, East Lothian, Scotland, late 1942 (sequential photos 81–84). Preparing for an oath of allegiance ceremony with the colour party holding the regimental pennon (scarlet and orange with a thin central black stripe). With the formation of 1st Polish Armoured Division in February 1942, its anti-tank element was 10th Anti-Tank Squadron. This was changed to the 1st Anti-Tank Regiment and renamed in 1944 as 1st Anti-Tank Artillery Regiment. (Richard Szczawinski)

82. Colour Party, Gosford House, near Longniddry, East Lothian, Scotland, late 1942. New recruits taking their oath of allegiance to their country by placing their right hand on a gun, which for Artillery represents the colour, which in this case is a British 6 pdr Anti-Tank. (Richard Szczawinski)

83. Gullane, Scotland, January 1943. General Sikorski, Commander-in-Chief and Prime Minister, visiting the Divisional Artillery regiments on a British Universal carrier belonging to 1st Motorised Artillery Regiment. The carrier was an open-topped armoured vehicle used for a wide range of battlefield and support roles and was often referred to, unofficially, as a 'Bren-gun' carrier. Note soldiers in parade order in the background. (Richard Szczawinski)

84. Gullane, Scotland, January 1943. A close up of the parade in photo 83. The artillery units consisted of 1st Motorised Artillery Regiment, 1st Anti-Tank Regiment and the Anti-Aircraft Battery, renamed from June 1943, 1st Anti-Aircraft Artillery Regiment. (Richard Szczawinski)

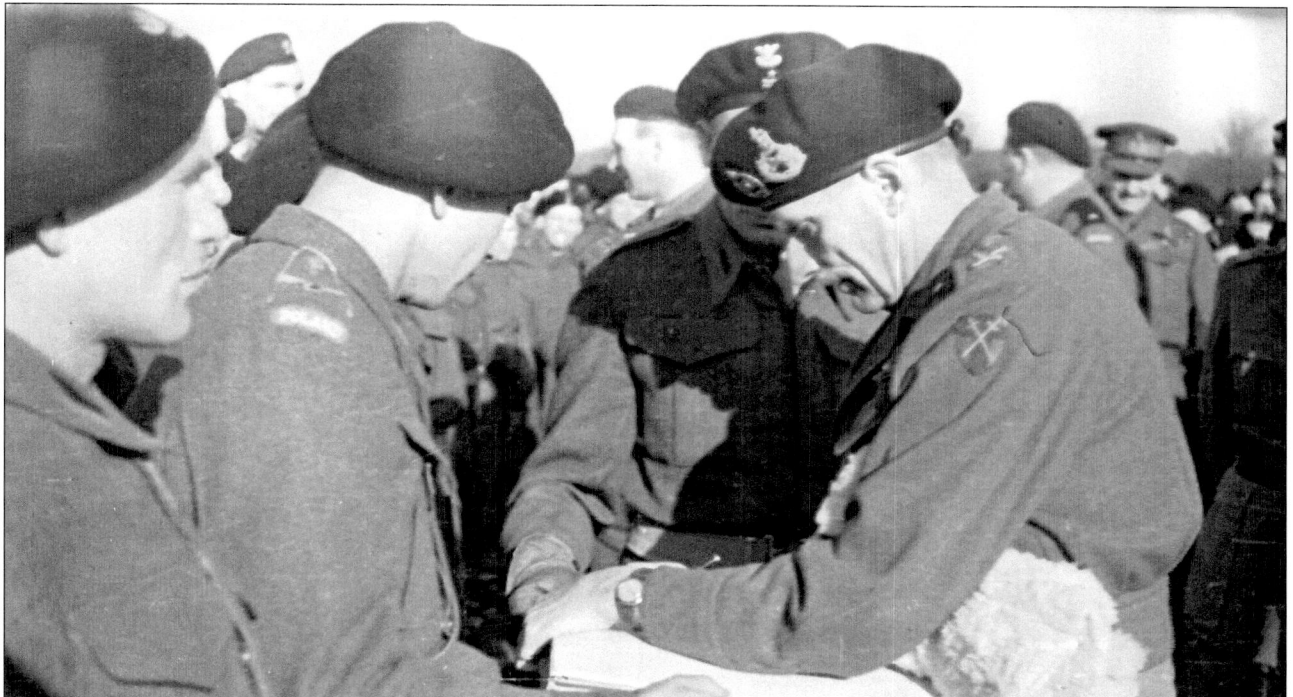

85. Kelso, Scotland, 13 April 1944 (sequential photos 85–89). General Montgomery (1887–1976) inspects the 1st Polish Armoured Division, providing him the opportunity to assess the readiness of the Division, meet its officers and give one of his celebrated inspirational speeches to the assembled troops in the run-up to D-Day. Here Monty is seen signing some sort of official visitors' volume of the 2nd Armoured Regiment with its commander Major Stanislaw Koszutski, having removed his dispatch rider's woollen gloves. He was a not a strict follower of British Army dress regulations, which puzzled and disappointed the awaiting troops. On his shoulder he wears the formation patch of 21st Army Group.

86. Kelso, Scotland, 13 April 1944. From the left are Major Stanisław Koszutski, commander of the 2nd Armoured Regiment, General Maczek, General Montgomery (Monty) wearing dispatch rider's woollen gloves and Colonel Tadeusz Majewski, commander of the 10th Armoured Cavalry Brigade. In 1940 Monty had been one of the first senior officers to wear battledress. His practice of wearing a Royal Tank Regiment (RTR) cap badge in addition to his General Officer's badge on his beret (the badge positioned to his right) originated in North Africa. Sometimes he substituted the RTR badge for that of the formation or unit he was visiting, although here the badge appears to be that of the RTR.

87. Kelso, Scotland, 13 April 1944. Continuing his inspection, Monty meets soldiers from an armoured unit, note British tankers' helmets. To his right is Colonel Majewski. To the right rear, wearing a Rogatywka is Brigadier-General Stanisław Sosabowski (1892–1967) commander of the 1st Polish Independent Parachute Brigade, numbering 3000 men, which was also inspected on the day. Formed on 23 September 1941, it was created to support the resistance in Poland, but in June 1944 it was incorporated into the Polish forces of the West, fighting notable at Arnhem in September 1944. Post-war, attached to the 1st Polish Armoured Division, the Brigade carried out occupational duties in Germany, until disbandment in June 1947. On the far left is Lieutenant General Janusz Głuchowski recently appointed Commander-in-Chief of Polish Army Forces in England, excluding the 1st Polish Independent Parachute Brigade, which reported directly to the Government-in-exile.

88. Kelso, Scotland, 13 April 1944. Monty makes his way past the colour parties and the Guard of Honour, immediately followed to his right by Colonel Majewski, General Maczek, Lieutenant General Józef Zając, Inspector of Training, Polish Armed Forces in the West, who commanded the Polish air defences in 1939 and was the CO in the Middle-East prior to General Anders and Lieutenant General Głuchowski, followed by an unknown officer.

89. Kelso, Scotland, 13 April 1944. In North Africa Monty had adopted the policy of addressing his men and briefing them as to their role in his forthcoming operations and is seen here continuing that process addressing the Division. He is recorded as saying 'We will go together, you and I, to kill the Germans'. He had returned to the United Kingdom in January 1944, after leading the 8th Army in Italy to take command of 21st Army Group, for the forthcoming Normandy invasion. General Maczek can be seen behind Monty holding his arm up to block the sun from his eyes.

90. Scotland circa 1942–43. Polish soldiers wearing their tankers crew helmets, patrolling through a Scottish town.

91. Location unknown, 1943. During its period of training in Great Britain the division was equipped with Crusader III and Covenanter III cruiser tanks (neither seeing operational service with the Poles). Here a trainload of Crusaders III are being transported by train mounted on the standard railway warflats, designed for the carriage of armoured vehicles. On the wagon in the centre are a number of Rotatrailers that carried fuel. These were designed to be towed by the tanks and could be detached before going into combat. (*With the Tanks of the 1st Polish Armoured Division*, K. Jamar and A.Tomaszewska; H.L. Smit and Z. Hengelo, Holland, 1946)

92. Kirkcudbright range. Scotland spring 1944 (sequential photos 92–98), located on the northern coastline of the Solway Firth in Dumfries and Galloway, near the town of Kirkcudbright. Stuart Mk V tanks and crew of the Division in training. All American vehicles received were painted in Olive Drab (no 9) paint, however the British used paint SCC NO 15 which was similar to Olive Drab, but slightly darker. This achieved some form of colour uniformity amongst Allied vehicles.

93. Kirkcudbright range. Scotland spring 1944. The Stuart Mk V tank had a crew of 4 and was used primarily in the reconnaissance role, with each armoured regiment allocated 11 Stuarts. Nicknamed 'Honeys' by the British, it mounted an ineffectual 37mm gun with poor armour protection and had become largely obsolete by the latter stages of the war in Europe.

94. Kirkcudbright range. Scotland spring 1944. The triangular marking on the side of the tank in the foreground denotes 'A' or 1st Squadron (a square for B or 2nd Squadron and a circle for C or 3rd Squadron).

95. Kirkcudbright range. Scotland spring 1944. The crewman on the extreme left is wearing the British (1935) black two-piece working dress only issued to armoured personnel, rarely seen at this stage of the war.

96. Kirkcudbright range. Scotland spring 1944. A long barrel rod is used by crewman to clean the rifling within the barrel, which was necessary daily, to ensure accuracy by preventing the build-up of dirt. Quite often under field conditions a cloth bag was tied onto the barrel end to keep it sealed, but removed in combat. A crewman can also be seen lowering the bow Browning M1919 machine-gun, having been stripped and cleaned into a hatch for re-instalment

97. Kirkcudbright range. Scotland spring 1944. Crew 'mount-up' ready to move off. The crewman seen leaning out of the turret, to the right, is Sergeant Jan Pirog.

98. Kirkcudbright range. Scotland spring 1944. A Stuart moves off the range.

99–105. Sherman V manual. Orange paperback booklet (16cm × 20.5cm). Translated from the British version, dated 1944, stating for official use only. Other volumes covered operation and maintenance. At full-strength an armoured regiment was allocated 56 Sherman V tanks.

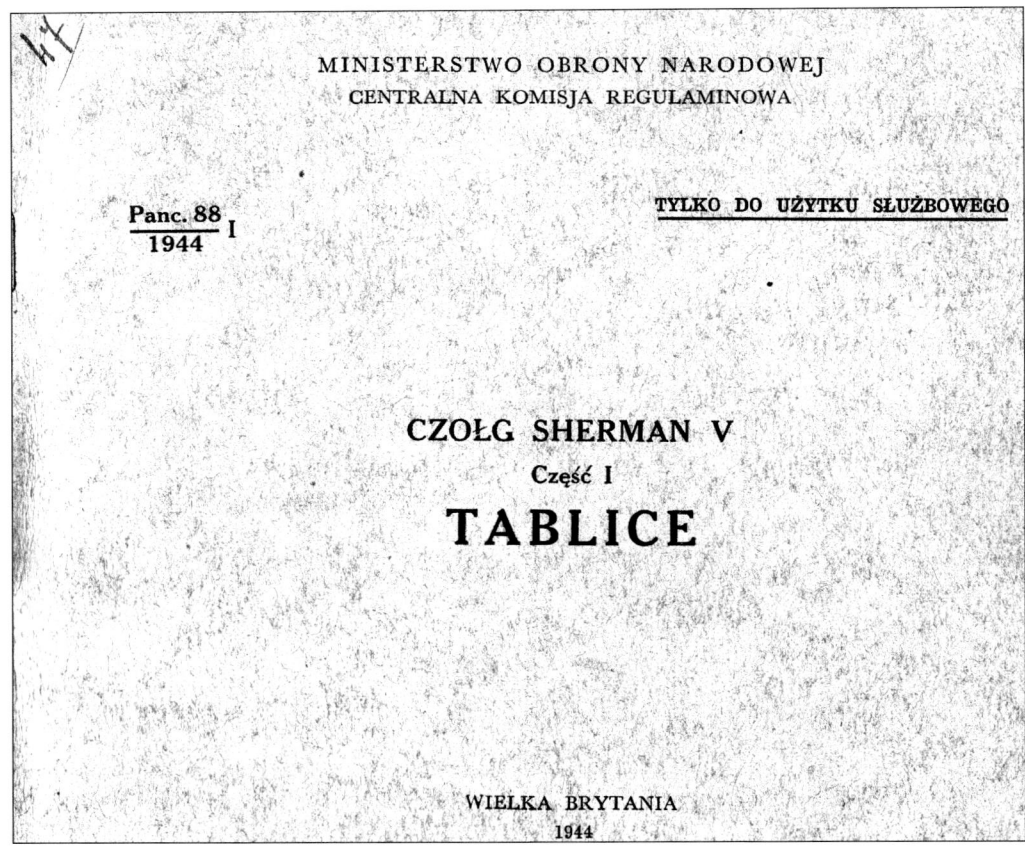

PART II: 1940-44   61

TABLICA 1.

WIDOK Z PRAWEJ STRONY

TABLICA 3.

WIDOK Z PRZODU

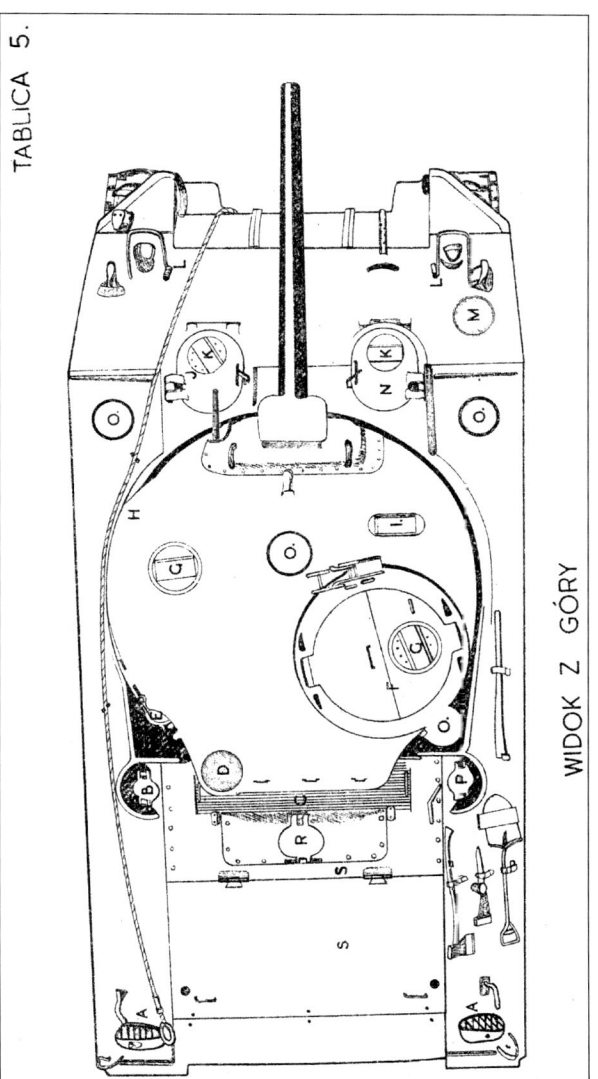

TABLICA 5.

WIDOK Z GÓRY

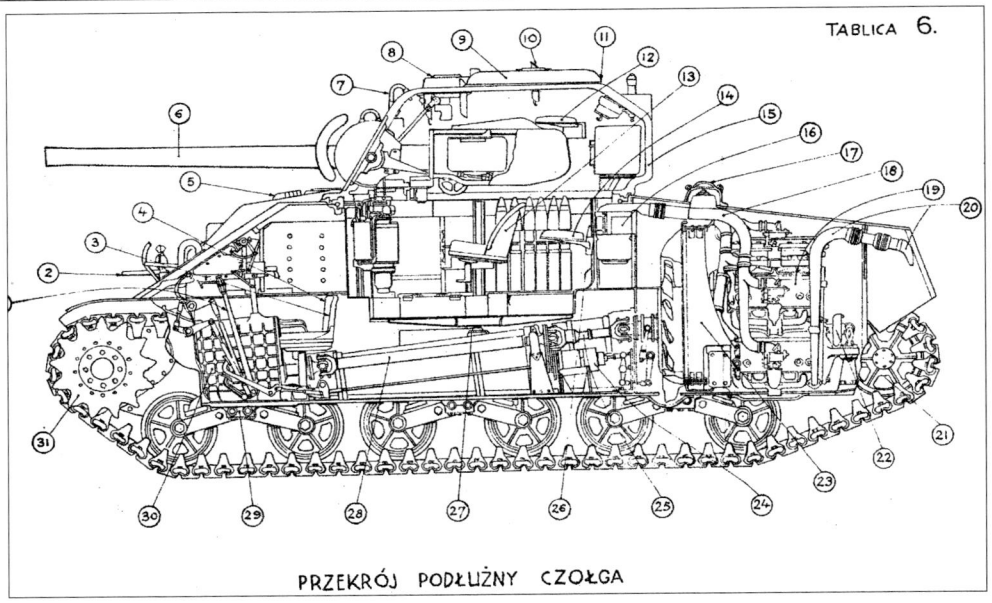

PRZEKRÓJ PODŁUŻNY CZOŁGA — TABLICA 6.

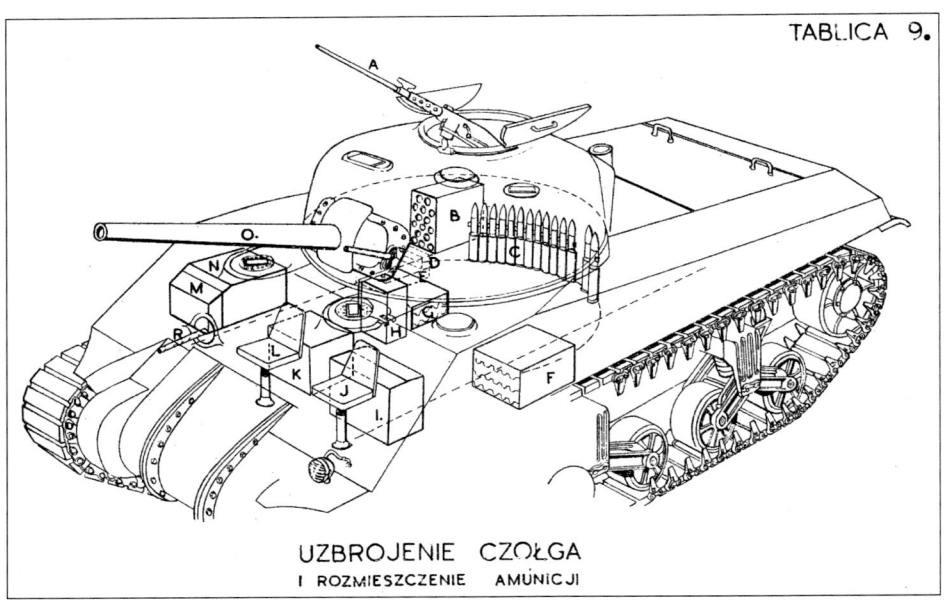

UZBROJENIE CZOŁGA I ROZMIESZCZENIE AMUNICJI — TABLICA 9.

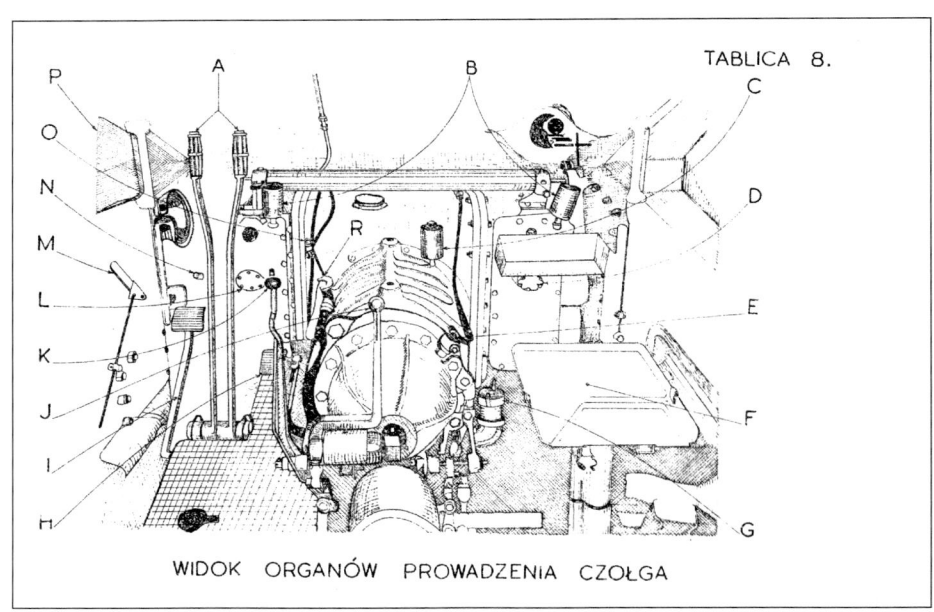

WIDOK ORGANÓW PROWADZENIA CZOŁGA — TABLICA 8.

Part III

1944–45

106. Normandy, France, August 1944. The Division forms up near Bayeux after landings at Arromanches-Les-Bains and Courseulles-sur-Mer, between late July and early August, as part of 2nd Canadian Corps. In the foreground is a Sherman VC Firefly (17 pounder) one of 12 allocated to each armoured regiment. *(With the Tanks of the Polish 1st Armoured Division, K.Jamar, A.Tomaszewska, Hengelo, Holland 1946)*

107. North-Western Europe, autumn 1944. A trench is prepared so a tank can be driven over the top, offering protection against aircraft attack and shrapnel from shell bursts (see photo 108). Markings, left to right, PL (Poland) 473 (Divisional Replacement Centre). Damaged vehicles would be repaired and stored until issue, 52 (2nd Armoured Regiment), Triangle (1st Squadron), Hussar Helmet (1st Armoured Division).

108. Normandy, France, August 1944. Crusader III, AA (anti-aircraft) Mk II tank, 2nd Armoured Regiment, one of six allocated per armoured regiment. With the significantly reducing threat from the German Luftwaffe the Crusader, with its 2 × 20mm Oerlikon cannon, was often used in the ground support-role with the infantry. Note the crewman, extreme left, has 'borrowed' an American M3 'Grease-gun' (so nicknamed as it resembled a mechanic's greaser tool) substituting the standard issue British Sten-gun, seen here without a magazine fitted, held by the crewman, third from left.

109. Normandy, France, August 1944. German losses in the Falaise pocket were very heavy in both equipment and personnel. A knocked-out German Pz.Kpfw V Panther (probably an Ausf.A). Top left, a divisional utility vehicle, note its PL marking. Resting on his vehicle is Captain Kamil Czarnecki of the 10th Mounted Rifles. (*1st Polish Armoured Division, 1 VIII 1944- 11 XI 1944, France-Belgium-Holland,* Drukkerijen Louis Vermijs N.V., Breda- Oosterhout)

110. Normandy, France August 1944. This photo shows two aspects of the German forces in Normandy. On the one hand, were its Panzer divisions, equipped with high quality, technologically advanced armoured vehicles, often superior to their Allied equivalents. The abandoned/knocked-out PzKw V Panther Ausf A on the left is in stark contrast to the two dead horses, still in the traces of their destroyed wagon, typical of the type of transport that supported the majority of the German infantry formations. (*1st Polish Armoured Division, 1 VIII 1944- 11 XI 1944, France-Belgium-Holland,* Drukkerijen Louis Vermijs N.V., Breda- Oosterhout)

111. Falaise pocket, Normandy, France, August 1944. Polish soldiers pick their way through shattered German equipment destroyed in the pocket. On the left is what remains of a German SdKfz 7/1, a 11.53 ton half-track mounting a four-barrelled 2cm Flakvierling 38, which can be seen amidst the wreckage and was used against both air and ground targets. The figure on the left is wearing the British 1943 issue tankers oversuit, nick-named the 'Pixie suit'. (*1st Polish Armoured Division, 1 VIII 1944- 11 XI 1944, France-Belgium-Holland,* Drukkerijen Louis Vermijs N.V., Breda- Oosterhout)

112. Elbeuf, France, 29 August 1944. A Polish Cromwell crossing the Seine near Elbeuf, on the Warsaw Bridge built by 10th and 11th Field Company Engineers, recognition signs 46 and 41 respectively. First to cross was the Divisional reconnaissance unit, 10th Mounted Rifle Regiment. Great effort had been put into the approaches of the Bailey bridge by the sappers of the Field Park Company, especially on the right bank to enable the motorised columns to connect to the main road leading to Neufchatel and Abbeville. The offensive was on, direction Pas de Calais and Belgium.
(*1st Polish Armoured Division, 1 VIII 1944- 11 XI 1944, France-Belgium-Holland,* Drukkerijen Louis Vermijs N.V., Breda- Oosterhout)

113. Belgium/Dutch border, autumn 1944. A Panzer IV/70 (V) lies abandoned, with a number of other vehicles on a road in north-western Europe. Based on a Panzer IV chasis, with added protection provided by the use of sloped armour and a low silhouette, this vehicle was an improved version of the Jagdpanzer IV. Introduced in August 1944 the Panzer IV/70 mounted the same 75mm gun as the PzKw V Panther. Behind can be seen the Marder featured in photo 114.

114. Belgium/Dutch border, autumn 1944. A German Panzerjäger (tank hunter) 38(t) 7.5cm, Pak40/3, Ausf H, Marder III, based on the obsolete Czech (CKD) LT vz.38 tank, and built from late 1942 to early 1943 to counter the ever increasing numbers of enemy tanks on the Eastern Front. This modified type had a different fighting compartment and the German PaK40 instead of the captured Soviet 7.62 cm gun, from its predecessor. This one appears to have broken down, note tow-ropes (refer to photo 113, as this is the same vehicle positioned behind the Jagdpanzer). The open fighting compartment left much to be desired as the crew were exposed to overhead bursts and aircraft strafing as well as the weather. Further the thin armour only offered minimal protection against small arms and the PaK40's huge muzzle blast exposed the vehicle's position so hit and run tactics had to be employed.

115. North-Western Europe, autumn 1944. A German Jagdpanther (Hunting Panther), a heavy German tank destroyer sits undamaged in an enemy vehicle collection point. Based on the Panther chassis, this one is a late production model (May 1944) with a sectional barrel for its 8.8cm Pak43.3 L/71. It had a low profile and was well armoured and successfully used both as a tank destroyer and a battle tank. Immediately behind to the left sits another Jagdpanther and in the background various other German tanks including a Panzer IV/70(V).

116. Baarle Nassau, Holland, 2 October 1944. A German Flugzeugabwehrkanone (Flak) anti-aircraft gun either a 88mm Flak 18 or 36 (also effective in the anti-tank role) from Heeres-Flak Abteilung 291 destroyed in action with Polish tanks.

117. North-Western Europe, autumn 1944. A knocked-out German Pak 43 88mm anti-tank gun on low silhouette mounting, one of its two axle limbers can be seen on the left. It had an effective range of 4000 metres which enabled penetration of heavily armoured Allied vehicles at long ranges, especially those encountered on the Eastern Front.

118. Thielt, Belgium, 8 September 1944. M10 Achilles, named 'Bydgoszcz' after one of the crew's hometown, of 2nd Battery, 1st Anti-Tank Artillery Regiment. The Achilles mounted the same 17 pdr as was fitted to the Sherman Firefly. Crewman Tadeusz Szczawinski top middle, Boleslaw Orzeschowski standing second right and Sergeant Jan Pirog standing on the first left. A special detachment was formed tasked with capturing the town, included elements of the 24th Lancers Regiment, 8th Rifles and one battery each from the Anti-Tank Regiment and the motorised artillery. This was only accomplished after heavy fighting and infantry reinforcements. (Richard Szczawinski)

119. Ruiselede Belgium, 8 September 1944. Tanks of 2nd Armoured Regiment, encircling Thielt, destroy a retreating German column caught in the open on a stretch of road covering 2 kilometres with both motorised and horse-drawn vehicles, inflicting heavy casualties. Later described by General Maczek as a 'small Chambois'. (*1st Polish Armoured Division, 1 VIII 1944- 11 XI 1944, France-Belgium-Holland,* Drukkerijen Louis Vermijs N.V., Breda- Oosterhout)

120. Ruiselede, Belgium, 8 September 1944. Part of the destroyed column, seen in photo 119. A German PAK 40 gun with a casualty lying in the foreground crater.

121. St.Niklaas, Belgium, 12 September 1944. The town was liberated by the 1st Armoured Regiment and some of its vehicles, including a Sherman tank, are seen parked on the main square with the town hall in the background. On 3 March 1946, the coat of arms along with the colours was presented to the regiment, whose members wore the insignia on their right sleeve. (*1st Polish Armoured Division, 1 VIII 1944- 11 XI 1944, France-Belgium-Holland,* Drukkerijen Louis Vermijs N.V., Breda- Oosterhout)

122. Belgium, September 1944. M10 and crew of 2nd Battery, 1st Anti-Tank Artillery Regiment with Boleslaw Orzeschowski, second left and Tadeusz Szczawinski, third from left. (Richard Szczawinski)

123. Holland, Axel, the Weststraat, 19 September 1944. A liberation parade is hosted by the local population and supported by the Division. Thanks to Gilles Lapers for identifying the location. (Richard Szczawinski)

124. Holland, 20 September 1944. Abandoned German 3.7cm Flak gun (possibly a Flak 43). Advancing from Ghent the Division captures Terneuzen clearing the south bank of the Scheldt, east of Antwerp.

125. Alphen, Holland, 5 October 1944. The Divisional attack on Alphen begins in the late morning. As enemy defences are overrun, German prisoners are searched and interrogated for any intelligence information, with various personal effects, once checked, discarded. Note the German MP40 Schmeisser 'liberated' by the Polish soldier positioned in the center of the photo. A Sherman tank can just be seen over the heads of the prisoners along with a jeep to the right.

126. Alphen, Holland, 5 October 1944. In the foreground is a Sherman MkV with 'applique' armour added to turret and hull side. Note Allied star has been toned-down to prevent it being used as a targeting point by enemy gunners. The tank in the background is a Sherman Firefly with its barrel disguised to conceal its length as they were a priority target for German gunners. After a fierce battle the town was finally taken that evening by 2nd Armoured Regiment, supported by 9th Rifle Battalion, after a wedge had been driven into the enemy defences, splitting their forces.

127. Alphen, Holland, 5 October 1944. Sherman Mk.V (M4A4), HQ Squadron (diamond sign) unit unidentified.

128. Holland, October 1944. M10 Achilles 'Bydgoszcz' of 2 Battery, 1st Anti-Tank Artillery Regiment. The crew stretch their legs with Tadeusz Szczawinski first right. (Richard Szczawinski)

129. Holland, October 1944. An M10 Achilles self-propelled anti-tank gun has come to grief in a Dutch field, much to the great interest of local children. It has been fitted with two Browning 0.30 calibre machine-guns. These were intended to provide close defence against German Panzerfaust and Panzerschreck anti-tank teams. The Panzerfaust (lit.'Tank Fist'), was a mass-produced portable disposable one-shot recoilless anti-tank weapon, in-service from late 1943. Range varied from 60–100 metres with its warhead penetrating most Allied tanks. The Panzerschreck (lit. 'Tank terror') was a reusable light-weight rocket launcher with an effective range of 150 metres. It was similar in design to the Allied ' bazooka '. Also note the use of tracks as additional armour protection.

130. Breda, Holland, 28 October 1944. Prisoners captured before Breda by 10th Mounted Rifle Regiment. An outflanking manoeuvre by the Division causes the Germans to withdraw from Breda with minimal damage inflicted and minor civilian casualties. This is followed by the advance northwards, over the River Mark and canal, towards Moerdijk to capture bridges over the Maas.

131. Breda, Holland October 1944. Polish vehicles parked near the Church of our Lady, including a Ford WOA 2 in the foreground and an Austin K2 Ambulance to the left. Honorary insignia was worn by 8th Rifle Battalion, 3rd Rifle Brigade. (*1st Polish Armoured Division, 1 VIII 1944- 11 XI 1944, France-Belgium-Holland,* Drukkerijen Louis Vermijs N.V., Breda- Oosterhout)

132. Breda, Holland, October 1944. M10 Achilles, 2nd Battery, 1st Anti-Tank Artillery Regiment. Crewman Boleslaw Orzeschowski poses with the Kruis family, left to right, Paul and his wife Riek with children Ger and Ellie sitting on the Achilles with an unidentified female with Boleslaw. Research by Gilles Lapers has reunited the family Kruis with the son of the photographer, Richard Szczawinski. (Richard Szczawinski)

133. Mark Canal, Holland, 1 November 1944. In the background lies a destroyed bridge over the canal. An Achilles M10 moves past two Bren-gun carriers, one of which is burning. A bridgehead was established over the canal by 8th Rifles, reinforced by a squadron of 2nd Armoured Regiment. However due to repeated heavy enemy attacks and mounting losses, a withdrawal is ordered and carried out in the evening with covering fire from Divisional artillery.

134. Mark Canal, Holland, 2 November 1944 (sequential photo 134–135). Knocked out Sherman V, 2nd Armoured Regiment. Crewmen observe the damaged tank. A new bridgehead is established in the area of Aalst and Vraggelen enabling the whole Division to cross.

135. Mark Canal, Holland, 2 November 1944. Sergeant-Major A.L. Jarzembowski, 'A' Squadron, 2nd Armoured Regiment (standing right) converses with another crew member over their lucky escape as their Sherman was penetrated just above the ball-mounted front machine-gun. The Sherman had a tendency to ignite easily when penetrated and burn furiously, hence its German nick-name ' Tommy cooker'. Note 473 marking (1st Field delivery Squadron) left of arm of service sign 52.

136. Terheijden, Holland, 5 November 1944. Shermans including MkIIAs, park up under the two hundred year old cornmill *'De Arend'* (the Eagle), which was used by the Germans as an observation post. The town was captured by 9th Rifles and 24th Lancers Regiment after heavy fighting.

137. Zevenbergschen Hoek, Holland 5 November 1944. The St. Bartholomeus church appears largely intact. The town was captured by 2nd Armoured Regiment and elements of 3rd Infantry Brigade.

138. Zevenbergschen Hoek, Holland, 5 November 1944. The St. Bartholomeus church, badly damaged during the fighting, was demolished post-war and rebuilt on a much smaller scale.

139. North of Breda, Holland, November 1944. A knocked-out Sturmgeschütz (StuG) III Ausf. G assault gun belonging to Heeres-Sturmartillerie-Brigade 667 (assault artillery). Note unit insignia, a unicorn on a shield. Sturmgeschutz Abteilung 667 was formed in Germany in June 1942 and transferred to the Eastern Front, where it was virually wiped out during the Soviet summer offensive of 1944. Withdrawn to the Netherlands to be rebuilt, the unit, now renamed, was assigned to Kampfgruppe (Battlegroup) Chill (Generalleutnant Kurt Chill, commander 85th Infantry Division) and was in Breda, mid-October. The unit remained active across Holland and Western Germany until the war's end. The StuG was initially devised as an infantry artillery support vehicle dealing with enemy defence positions, but increasing used as a anti-tank weapon as the war progressed. Variants were built throughout the war. This late war production tank has damaged Schürzen plates, side skirts fitted as additional armour and has had concrete used either side of the 'Saukopf'(pig's head) gun mantlet, as additional protection (questionable) from anti-tank shells. As there were no Panzer Divisions deployed in this sector most enemy armour encountered were assault guns and self-propelled anti-tank guns.

140. Holland, November 1944. Destroyed canal bridge. German defensive tactics included the destroying of any crossings over the numerous rivers, canals and dykes as well as deliberate flooding to prevent enemy movement. This resulted in inevitable delays to the advance, as the engineers built suitable bridging and it also created extensive detours, often frustratingly counter-productive, as alternative routes were sought by the leading elements of the Division.

141. Holland, November 1944. Polish crewman, top left, in 'Pixie suit' tank overalls, inspecting German casualties. Note Parachute helmet on central lying figure, indicating a soldier from a Fallschirmjäger (Paratroop) unit.

142. Holland, November 1944. German prisoners sit on the ground in front of a captured camouflaged German Army Mercedes bus, note white flag hanging above front wheel arch. Patriotic graffiti has been applied to the bus including on the panel above the windscreen and sides. The graffiti refer to the three children of exiled Queen Juliana, Beatrix, Irene and Margriet. A Sherman MkIIA can be seen top right with a M5 half-track on the left.

143. Moerdijk, Holland, 6 November 1944. Knocked-out German StuG III Ausf.G with 'saukopf' ('pig's head') gun mantlet, The objective was to capture the bridges at the Hollandsche Diep, estuary of the Rhine and Waas rivers. The area was heavily defended and protected by concrete blocks and bunkers forming part of the German defences on the Waas.

144. Maas river, Holland, November 1945. Sherman 'Hybrid' (tank using an M4 composite hull) Firefly of the 2nd Armoured Regiment shelling enemy positions. Following the capture of Moerdijk, the south bank of the Maas was now held by the Allies.

145. Holland, November/December 1944. Sherman MkIIAs pause on a road with foreground crew consulting a map. Note muddy conditions compounded by bad weather and deliberate damage to dykes and drainage systems by the enemy.

146. Raamsdonk, River Maas, Holland, December 1944 (sequential photos 146-148). Destroyed German tanks (including a StuG IIIG) and reconnaissance vehicles (from schnelle Abteilung 505) of the 256.Volks-grenadier Division, defending the last stronghold at Raamsdonk village, defending the Mass crossing at the Keizersveer bridge, 3 miles north of the village.

147. Raamsdonk, River Maas, Holland, December 1944. Another knocked-out German StuG III (type unknown).The sector covered by the Division is increased to 50km due to Allied regrouping following the German Ardennes Offensive on 16 December 1944.

148. Raamsdonk, River Maas, Holland, December 1944. A knocked out German Sonderkraftfahrzeug (Sd.Kfz) 10 half-track mounting a 2cm Flak, one of five from schnelle Abteilung 505. Operation COIN was fought on 31 October by the 7th Battalion Black Watch and tanks from 'C' Squadron Northamptonshire Yeomanry, resulting in the loss of five British and eight German vehicles. The stubborn German resistance resulted in a successful withdrawal by their troops before the bridge was blown, preventing its capture. Ordered to dig-in on the southern bank of the Maas, many Poles took the opportunity to have their photo taken on this battlefield.

149. Winter 1944–1945, on the Maas. A group of soldiers from 1st Anti-Tank Artillery Regiment pose for the camera on a M10 Achilles. Tadeusz Szczawinski is seen on the first left. In late December offensive patrols and sorties were conducted by both sides. In the New Year the sector held by the Division was reduced progressively to 15km by March 1945. The Poles were not only bored but waited impatiently as the Allies crossed the Rhine in Operations PLUNDER and VARSITY 23-24 March 1945. Then on 6 April 1945 battle orders were received and the Division moved to the Hengelo area of Holland, their dispersal point, after an 18 hour forced march. Direction Tilburg, s'Hertogenbosch, Gennep, Goch, Rees then back across the border into Holland, then northwards and into Germany towards Emden. During this period the Division was assigned to the Canadian II Corps. (Richard Szczawinski)

150. Raamsdonk, River Maas, Holland, early 1945. Two Polish soldiers pose on a knocked-out German StuG III Ausf G (see photos 146-148) with one of them holding one of the assault gun's 75 mm shells. Note left-side track is missing.
(Richard Szczawinski)

151. Gennep, Holland 7 April 1945. Near the Dutch-German border. Polish jeeps, possibly Military Police, drive through the town cleared of rubble.

152. Dutch-German border, April 1945. Resistance hardens. With the fighting ended, dismounted crewmen inspect the battlefield with German casualties scattered on the ground. Note to the bottom left, an unused Panzerfaust. The Germans defending the area included remnants of 6th and 8th Fallschirmjäger (Parachute) divisions. The 6th had been raised in France in 1944, seen heavy fighting in Normandy and had withdrawn to Holland for rebuilding. The 8th was a newly raised division, formed in January 1945

153. Dutch-German border, 9 April 1945. Customs signage on the route from Gennep towards Goch in Germany.

154. Dutch-German Border, 9 April 1945. Crossing into Germany, soldiers of the 2nd Armoured Regiment pose before a warning sign, left to right, unidentified soldier, Lieutenant Wladyslaw Kulesza and Lieutenant Janusz Barbarski. Note Canadian formation sign on notice-board, top left.

155. Rees, Germany, 9 April 1945 (sequential photos 155–156). Pontoon Bailey bridge crossing on the Rhine near Rees. The Division crosses through Germany then back onto Dutch soil with the advance towards Terborg-Emden.

156. Rees, Germany, 9 Arpil 1945. View from the same bridge overlooking the destroyed town.

157. Germany, April 1945. A Humber Scout Car, Liaison Platoon, 2nd Armoured Regiment. A British designed light armoured car produced 1942–1945, the car had a crew of two, armed with two Bren guns with a top speed of 62 mph. Positioned behind is a M5 half-track with an Allied air recognition sign of a circled star.

158. Bourtange, Holland 15 April 1945. Tanks of the recently formed Battle Group (1) consisting of units from 10th Mounted Rifle Regiment and 10th Dragoon Regiment, supported by motorised artillery, were tasked with a reconnaissance towards Emmen. Bourtange, taken after 2 days fierce fighting, had been a strongly held defensive position reinforced with trenches. On the right a Sherman Mk V, a rarity in the Division at this stage as most of its tanks had been replaced by the MkIIA 76mm. A number of Mk V's and Fireflies also being 'retained'. At the top left a Sherman Mk IIA advances.

159. Holland, 1945. Knocked-out Soviet ZiS-3 76.2 mm field gun, often used by the Germans, in the anti-tank role, from captured Eastern Front equipment.

160. Germany, April 1945. On the way to Rhede, just over the Dutch border.

161. Holland, April 1945 (sequential photos 161–162). A long column of Sherman Mk IIAs, 2nd Armoured Regiment. The image shows the open nature of the local terrain providing excellent 'fields of fire' for enemy defenders.

162. Holland, April 1945. A close up of the column seen in photo (161). Sherman Mk IIAs, 2nd Armoured Regiment, lead a column along a Dutch road. Note hulls and turrets drapped with camouflage netting and canvas.

163. Holland, April 1945. German prisoners stop to have their photo taken, much to the distain of the observing Polish crewman in his Pixie suit. In the background stands a Sherman Mk IIA.

PART III: 1944–45   93

164. Rhede, Germany 16 April 1945 (sequential photos 164–172). Sherman Mk IIAs come to a halt amid burning buildings and woodland, during the advance towards Rhede.

165. Rhede, Germany 17 April 1945. Command element of one of the recently formed battle groups, attacking Rhede. A Sherman Mk IIA from 2nd Armd. Regiment and a M5 half-track from 10th Dragoons. Just visible beyond the M5 is another half-track with an extended canvas top (the white on the canvas top being the Allied star for air recognition), providing additional head-room for observation and radio equipment. This probably belonged to the Divisional Signal Battalion, which would explain the number of despatch riders seen.

166. Rhede, Germany 17 April 1945. Another Sherman Mk IIA pulls in behind the tank in photo 165.

167. Rhede, Germany 17 April 1945. Soldiers of 10th Dragoons flushing out the enemy on foot supported by 2nd Armoured Regiment. Note British Mark II 'Brodie' steel helmet on the turret.

168. Rhede, Germany 17 April 1945. Dramatic photo of a Sherman and exposed crew covered in smoke from a nearby building on fire, extreme right (see photo 169).

169. Rhede, Germany 17 April 1945. Same building as in previous photo 168, set alight to flush out the enemy, note Polish soldier on extreme left.

170. Rhede, Germany 17 April 1945. British Austin K2 'Katie' ambulances, so-called because of the War Office 'K2' designation, servicing an advanced Field Dressing Station. Divisional medical support was provided by 10th Light and 11th Heavy Field Ambulance Companies supported by the 1st Field Dressing Station and the 1st Field Hygiene Platoon. A Sherman is parked amongst smouldering ruin.

171. Rhede, Germany 17 April 1945. The local church remains intact amongst the ruins. The town was captured after fierce fighting against various German units including a naval infantry battalion, which resulted in its annihilation.

172. Rhede, Germany 17 April 1945. Escorted German prisoners make their way to the rear past a Polish armoured column.

173. Küsten Canal, Germany, 19 April 1945. Destroyed bridge blown by the Germans. Infantry of 9th Rifles launched an attack over the canal in assault boats, supported by a heavy artillery and air bombardment, which included rocket-firing Typhoons. Later on the same day, a rapidly built bridge by engineers of 10th Field Company, enabled armour to cross in force, including the 1st Armoured Regiment.

174. Lieutenant Colonel Stanisław Koszutski, German border area, April 1945. Commander of 2nd Armoured Regiment (28 April 1942 to 29 April 1945) is seen here with an RAF Air Liaison Officer, prior to handing over the command of the regiment to Major M. Gutowski (10th Mounted Rifle Regiment), who held the command until 10 June 1947. Koszutski was part of the patrol, along with 10 others including Lieutenant Janusz Barbarski and Lieutenant Doctor Władysław Kulesza which liberated Polish women prisoners at Stalag VI C, Oberlangen, on 12 April 1945.

175. German border area, April 1945. Lieutenant Janusz Barbarski, leaning on a Sherman Mk V turret and Lieutenant Doctor Władysław Kulesza, right foreground, show off their teddy bear mascot. Note spare tank idler wheels secured to the glacis plate and tracks to the sides of the turret and hull to upgrade the armour against anti-tank weapons.

176. Germany, April 1945. A German Panzer IV/70 (V), tank destroyer with 'Schürzen' side skirts lays apparently intact and abandoned in the area of the Kusten Canal. The tank was produced from mid-1944 to April 1945.

177. Stapelmoorer Heide, Germany, April 1945. Shermans of 3rd Squadron, 2nd Armoured Regiment. Recently captured German prisoners sit and await escort to the rear amongst Shermans in laager formation (a defensive formation with all guns pointing outwards). The Sherman in the left foreground is a Firefly and has a "trompe l'oeil (deceive the eye) painted out barrel. This was done to deceive the enemy into thinking that the shortened barrel meant a less powerful gun and therefore shorter range. This led to 'a false sense of security' with the enemy readily exposing itself, before engaging. The Sherman on the right appears to have been fitted with a Panzer Mk IV storage box on the rear of its turret. Taking advantage of 'captured' livestock, a goat is milked behind the Sherman on the right.

178. Germany, April 1945. Destroyed German Flak 3.7 anti-aircraft gun on cruciform mount.

179. Cromwell IV Cruiser Tank, Germany 1945. The tank first saw action in Normandy and was issued to British armoured reconnaissance units and equipped the 7th Armoured Division in its entirety. The tank had a 75mm British gun (OQF), good armour protection and with its powerful engine it could travel up to 40 miles per hour. The Division's armoured reconnaissance regiment, 10th Mounted Rifle Regiment (10th PSK) was the only unit equipped with the tank. Note additional track links welded to the hull to reinforce armour protection. In November 1944 the unit was reinforced by the arrival of a number of 17pdr equipped British Cruiser Mk VIII Challenger tanks.

180. Germany, 1945. M10 Achilles, 2nd Battery, 1st Anti-Tank Artillery Regiment. The turret is traversed for road or rail movement. Crewman Tadeusz Szczawinski is on the left, speaking into a mircophone, wearing a US Army issue tankers protective helmet, while his colleague on the right wears the standard issue British tankers helmet with the Polish national emblem on the front. Track links welded onto hull as additional armour protection. (Richard Szczawinski)

181. Hesel, Germany, 1 May 1945. The commander of a German Fallschirmjager unit arranging their surrender. Seen in the background is Lieutenant Wiatrowski's Sherman Mk IIA, HQ Squadron, 2nd Armoured Regiment. Note the jumping cow insignia drawn on the hull side of his tank (see photo 214)

182. Hesel, Germany, April 1945. Captured German Fallschirmjagers (Paratroops) on their way to the rear, passing Shermans of 2nd Armoured Regiment with Lieutenant Janusz Barbarski smoking a cigarette, leading the way.

183. Germany, May 1945. A Sexton self-propelled gun, mounting a 25pdr gun, built by the Canadians, from 1943 onto M4A1 Sherman chassis. Used in Normandy and throughout the North-West European campaign as indirect artillery support. The first vehicle in the column is named 'Jordanow', 2nd Battery, 1st Motorised Artillery Regiment.

PART III: 1944–45   103

184. Germany, May 1945. German prisoners being inspected by Major Michał Gutowski and Captain Władysław Jakubiec, 2nd Armoured Regiment.

185. Germany, May 1945. An Engineers column with the vehicle in the foreground a 4 ton 6 x6 Diamond T 967 with folding boat equipment. The next truck in line looks like a 3 ton 4 × 4 Ford V8 (F60L) and the two in the front of the convoy appear to be 4 ton 6 × 6 Diamond T975s.

186. Gross-Oldendorf, Germany 1 May 1945. Sherman Mk IIAs, 2nd Armoured Regiment pass a knocked out German 88mm gun on a wheeled mounting. The area had been cleared by the 10th (PSK) the Divisional armoured reconnaissance unit, advancing on Remels and then onto Westerstede.

187. Westerstede, Germany, 3 May 1945. A column of Sherman Mk IIAs pause in a German village, on the approach to Weterstede. All the crew are wearing the British issue armoured vehicle coveralls nicknamed "Pixie Suits".

188. Westerstede, Germany 3 May 1945. Polish troops in the town square with Stuart Mk V light reconnaissance tanks. To the left are M5 half-tracks with canvas covers. The banner on the building 'Hilfskrankenhaus' refers to a temporary or emergency hospital with the adjacent symbol unidentified. There appear to be two individuals in white coats at the end of the street, on the extreme right.

189. Bredchorn, Germany, 5 May 1945. A Staghound Mk I joins a convoy. It was an American design used by British and Canadian forces in the reconnaissance role, mounting a 37mm M6 gun . A half-track is just visible on the left. The dumped ordnance in the foreground would appear to be inert as there appears to be no warning signs. The Germans used surplus aircraft ordnance as mines and 'booby-traps' to blow bridges and roads. The two vehicles before the Staghound have the recognition sign 44 which is the Postal Service!

190. Leer, Germany, 5 May 1945. Last bridge of the war. The 3rd Canadian Infantry Division gained a crossing across the river Leda enabling the last bridge of the war, completed at 07.59 hours, to be built by Canadian II Corps engineers. The ceasefire came into effect at 08.00 hours so the claim is justified.

191. Germany, May 1945. Allied vehicle column (sequential photos 191–192). The vehicle on the right foreground is a 3 ton 4 × 4 GS Ford F60L, possibly Canadian-built. Note that the Allied recognition star is at an angle as this was often used by the Canadian Army to distinguish their vehicles from those of their America and British allies. Behind the Ford is a 4 ton 6 × 6 Diamond T975. A Stuart tank is just seen to the right with one of its crew greeting liberated French prisoners. Several camps were overrun by the Division, notably at Oberlangen on 12 April 1945.

192. Germany, May 1945. A Cromwell tank of 1st Squadron, 10th Mounted Rifle Regiment, moves off pass a column seen in photo 191. Note spare road wheel hanging from turret side.

193. Germany, May 1945. Abandoned German gun emplacement.

194–195. Germany May, 1945. A shot-up train discovered near Wilhelmshaven, possibly at Sengwarden, dubbed "Dönitz's Train" by the Poles. Note the German eagle on coach bodywork. There was a 'Sonderzug' (Special train) named 'Atlantik' which was used to bring staff from Sengwarden, about 8 miles north of Wilhelmshaven, to the Schleswig-Hostein command bunkers.

PART III: 1944–45   109

196. Varrelbusch Advanced Landing Ground (ALG) B113, Germany, May 1945. Flag pole with national colours, on the left, RAF and Belgian with Polish and Dutch on right. The central triangular flag is to indicate that the Commanding Officer is in residence. Squadrons: 302 (Polish), 317 (Polish), 322 (Dutch), 349 (Belgian).

197. Varrelbusch, Germany, May 1945. Allied airfield signage. This was Advanced Landing Ground (ALG) B113, where 131 (Polish) Wing was located from April until September and then moving to Ahlhorn. It was part of RAF 84 Group, 2nd Tactical Air Force. Post war, the Wing became part of the British Air Forces of Occupation (BAFO) and was eventually disbanded along with other Polish Air Force Units by January 1947. Its main operational role was 'Interdiction', the act of disrupting and destroying enemy supply routes by attacking roads, bridges, railways, supply depots and any means of transport by air, road, rail and water. The signs include 411 R.S.U. (RAF Repair and Servicing Unit), 408 ASP (RAF Air Stores Park), 84 GP RAF Police. The central German sign for Friesoythe, which has had graffiti applied, is about 13 miles north-west.

198. Varrelbusch, Germany, May 1945. Spitfire Mk IXs of 317 (Polish) Squadron code JH, an element of 131 Polish Wing. The aircraft wear the standard RAF camouflage and markings with Polish markings on the nose under the exhaust. The Squadron was re-equipped with the Spitfire XVI in May 1945. In late 1945, this aircraft was one of three Spitfires sent to Poland for an RAF exhibition. Although two of the Spitfires were exhibited publicly in Warsaw for a number of years they were eventually removed and allegedly destroyed as they were deemed ''not politically correct''.

199. Varrelbusch, Germany, May 1945. This Spitfire is an Mk LFXVIe Merlin-powered version, registration TD238 of No.302 (Polish) Squadron, fitted with a 'tear-drop' cockpit canopy which increased pilot visibility and armed with 20mm cannon and Browning 0.50 calibre machine guns.

200. Advance to Wilhelmshaven, Germany, 6 May 1945 (sequential photos 200–220). Following the surrender of all German forces on 4 May 1945 in North-West Europe, with the ceasefire declared for 08.00 hours on 5 May 1945, Major-General Stanisław Maczek was given the order to occupy Wilhelmshaven, the largest German Kreigsmarine (Navy) base, by Lieutenant-General Guy Simmonds, commanding Canadian II Corps. This was then relayed to Colonel Antoni Grudziński, commander of 10th Armoured Cavalry Brigade, to form a battle group to take the surrender on 6 May 1945. This was made up of the 2nd Armoured Regiment and 9th Rifle Battalion. Shermans Mk IIAs of the H.Q. Squadron (Diamond tactical sign painted yellow on turret) move off, with Major Gutowski's Sherman upfront.

201. On the road to Wilhelmshaven, Germany, 6 May 1945. The battle group, formed into two columns in full battle-drill order, was escorted by a German Army Officer as a guide through the fortress's defensive positions, which included minefields. Sherman Mk IIAs are seen negotiating railway rolling stock used as road barricades.

202. Wilhelmshaven, Germany, 6 May 1945. Major Michał Gutowski, commanding officer of 2nd Armoured Regiment, at the city limits, beside his Sherman Mk IIA, HQ Squadron.

203. Wilhelmshaven, Germany, 6 May 1945. The battle group forms up at the city limits at the junction of Bismarckstrasse and Schaarreihe. A message is sent to the German authorities to meet at these crossroads. The lead Sherman, Mk IIA, has an Allied air recognition sign of a circled star on top of its turret. Behind the tank are Humber Scout Cars.

204. Wilhelmshaven, Germany, 6 May 1945. A crewman of a Humber Scout Car of 2nd Armoured Regiment waits patiently in the rain at the crossroads, along with the German military escort who wear white armbands. Although both appear to be from the Heer (Army) a Waffen-SS registered motorbike has been used to escort the battle group. The scout car is armed with a Bren gun which is fitted to a Parrish-Lakeman Mounting (P.L.M.) which allowed the gun to be fired from within the vehicle using a system of strings attached to motorcycle-like handlebars. The mounting had been originally designed to hold anti-aircraft machine-guns fitted to tank turrets. Behind the Humber, is the Sherman MkIIA can be also be seen in photo 203.

205. Wilhelmshaven, Germany, 6 May 1945. The German delegation arrive and around noon the surrender is accepted by Colonel Grudziński with Divisional photographers recording the scene as it unfolds. Major Gutowski is the centre figure in the background, facing the camera. Note the armoured column on the extreme left is the one seen in photo 203.

206. Wilhelmshaven, Germany, 6 May 1945. The German surrender delegation, left to right Kapitän zur See Walter Mulsow, commander of Wilhelmshaven garrison, Ferdinand Heske, Chief of Police, Bernd Horstmann, NSDAP-Kreisleiter (National Socialist German Workers' Party District Head), Dr. Wilhem Müller, Mayor and Georg Seiffe, city administrator. The last three delegates decided wisely not to wear their Nazi party uniforms. A translator can just be seen behind Mulsow.

207. Wilhelmshaven, Germany, 6 May 1945. Colonel Antoni Grudziński consults a map with Kapitän zur See Mulsow. Major Gutowski stands on Grudziński's left.

208. Wilhelmshaven, Germany, 6 May 1945. Amid the ruins a street barricade has been partially cleared to allow access.

209. Wilhelmshaven, Germany, 6 May 1945. Rubble strewed side streets awaiting clearance.

210. Wilhelmshaven, Germany, 6 May 1945. German prisoners. Over 34,000 personal were captured and disarmed.

211. Wilhelmshaven, Germany, 6 May 1945. Following the surrender, Grudzinski's battle group moves into town and establishes a base at the Admiral von Schröder barracks. Sherman Mk IIAs, 2nd Armoured Regiment, are seen parked on the parade ground, in front of Block 2. A Sherman Armoured Recovery Vehicle (ARV) can be seen to the right rear, against the barrack building. Built in 1912, and originally called the Muhlenweg Barracks, it was renamed in 1936 after a First World War Admiral.

212. Wilhelmshaven, Germany, 6 May 1945. German prisoners, carrying bedding as they relocate quarters, pass crewmen of a Sherman Mk IIA, 2nd Armoured Regiment, parked on the parade ground of the barracks.

213. Wilhelmshaven, Germany, May 1945. Office building for 'Die Deutsche Arbeitsfront' (DAF), the German Labour Front, established in 1933 to replace the banned old trade unions and provided Party control over workers by offering employment, social security as well as leisure programmes. Located on Bismarckstraße 185, the building was originally used by Kuhlman, a company providing the Wehrmacht with precision engineered mechanical equipment. To avoid potential destruction by Allied bombing, the company was evacuated to Silesia, whereupon the building was taken over by the DAF. To the left can be seen a partially covered warning sign, stating that looting will be punished by death, signed by the Head of Police.

214. Wilhelmshaven, Germany, May 1945. Major Gutowski wearing a USAAF (United States Army Air Forces) issue leather flying jacket, communicates by radio in front of Lieutenant Wiatrowski's Sherman Mk IIA, HQ Squadron, 2nd Armoured Regiment, on the parade ground. Note the jumping cow insignia drawn on the tank side.

215. Wilhelmshaven, Germany, May 1945. Tank crews carrying out routine maintenance on their Sherman Mk IIAs, 2nd Armoured Regiment, parked on the parade ground, in front of Block 2, Admiral von Schröder barracks. Note the tank with the 'jumping cow' insignia, seen in photo 214.

216. Wilhelmshaven, Germany, May 1945. Sherman Mk IIAs of 2nd Armoured Regiment parked on the parade ground, Admiral von Schröder barracks. Note central figure wearing a highly coveted USAAF issue leather flying jacket.

217. Wilhelmshaven, Germany, May 1945 (sequential photos 217–219). Barrack rooftop view of the parade ground with parked vehicles of the 2nd Armoured Regiment. German prisoners with their belongings are grouped centrally by a goal-post, lower right. Note Armoured Recovery Vehicle (ARV) in front of jeeps, to the right of the barrack arched entrance, top left. From August 1944 an ARV was added to the 4th Platoon, 3rd Squadron of each armoured regiment. Also a Sherman Dozer, equipped with a bull dozer blade, can be seen on the extreme right row of tanks, second from top. A Dozer was assigned to each regiments' 4th Platoon.

218. Wilhelmshaven, Germany, May 1945. Another rooftop view showing the tanks parked on the parade ground. A Sherman Firefly with reversed turret in travel position can be seen at the foot of the photo and a Bedford QL truck with an air recognition star on its cab roof, to its left. The fourth tank from the bottom, has crewman having lifted the hatch, inspecting the engine. Also under the white canvas, top left, is a Sherman ARV. The Sherman at the top right is the same tank that is seen in photo 217, bottom right.

219. Wilhelmshaven, Germany, May 1945. Rooftop view of the parade ground with German and Allied vehicles. The front row of Allied trucks appear to be 3 ton 4 × 4 Bedford QLs GS (various models) with the seventh truck a 3 ton 4 × 4 Austin K5 GS. The smaller vehicles behind look like 15cwt 4 × 2 Bedford MWD GS. The central German vehicle, which appears white, is a Phanonman Granit truck.

PART III: 1944-45   121

220. Wilhelmshaven Port, Germany, May 1945. The huge port consisted of docks, shipyards and bases for U-boats and destroyers. The surrendered number of vessels totalled around 200 as well as 14 U-Boats with a further 23 discovered scuttled.

221. Jever, Germany, late May 1945 (sequential photos 221-234). The Division withdraws from Wilhelmshaven on 22 May to Jever airfield, designated Advanced Landing Ground (ALG) B-117, which had served primarily as a German nightfighter base. Note the remains of a giant Würzburg radar, named after a German city. The dish is lying in front and the operator's hut is on the ground to the rear. The Würzburg was a German gun-laying and early warning radar system which formed a vital component in the Luftwaffe's air defence network against RAF Bomber Command night raids on Germany. Würzburg radars guided German night fighters on to attacking bombers until the nightfighters own airborne systems were in range to detect the target. An early (smaller) version was captured by British paratroopers during Operation Biting at Bruneval in Northern France on the night of 27–28 February 1942. Later versions proved vulnerable to "window" jamming, the dropping of huge amounts of shredded tinfoil. After the war a number of captured systems were taken back to Great Britain and used in early experiments in radio astronomy.

222. Jever, Germany, 22 May 1945. Post-war the base was also used as a Displaced Persons camp until taken over by the RAF in 1952 and eventually returned to German control in 1961. In the foreground are 'BombenSchaltKasten' (BSK) which were incendiary bomb containers, appearing to hold 100 incendiaries.

223. Jever, Germany, 22 May 1945. An abandoned Luftwaffe Ju-88R nightfighter, fitted with early to mid-war Lichtenstein air-to-air radar with the 'Hirschgeweih' (stag's antlers) antennas installed on the nose.

224. Jever, Germany, 22 May 1945. Same aircraft as seen in photo 223.

225. Jever, Germany, late May 1945. A wrecked Junkers Ju-87 G2 markings T6+FH, with twin mounted 37mm anti-tank guns, one of which can be seen under the wing. Nicknamed the 'Kanonenvogel' (Cannon Bird). The 'Werknummer', the production number, can be seen on the tail above the Swastika. It was developed on the Eastern Front as a ground attack aircraft and only used against the ever-increasing Soviet armed forces. To avoid surrendering to the Soviets, a number of aircraft were flown to Allied-occupied airfields but patriotically damaged by carrying out a crash landing, knocking off the undercarriage and destroying the propeller. A sister-aircraft, T6+FU surrendered intact to the Americans at ALG 'R-11 Eschwege', which had been captured in early April 1945.

226. Jever, Germany, late May 1945. Rear view of aircraft seen in photo 225.

227. Jever, Germany, late May 1945. An abandoned and partially camouflaged Siebel Si 204 light communications aircraft sits outside a hangar.

228. Jever, Germany, late May 1945. Tail of a Ju 88R night fighter in a partially damaged wooden hangar.

229. Jever, Germany, late May 1945 (sequential photos 229–234). A British Army Auster AOP V carrying General Anders on a Divisional visit. These aircraft were used as airborne artillery observers and as liaison aircraft by senior officers.

230. Jever, Germany, late May 1945. Lieutenant General Władysław Anders, commander of the Polish 2nd Corps in Italy (1943–46) visiting the Division is greeted by General Klemens Rudnicki (Divisional commander from 21 May 1945 to 10 June 1946) accompanied right to left by Major General Mazcek, Lieutenant General Guy Simonds, commander of the Canadian II Corps, General John Tredinnick Crocker, Officer Commanding (OC) British I Corps, who commanded the 1st Polish Armoured Division from 28 September 1944 until 8 April 1945, when the Division reverted to Simonds' Canadian II Corps. Other personal unidentified.

231. Jever, Germany, late May 1945. Lieutenant General Anders addresses the Division alongside General Rudnicki and invited guests.

232. Jever, Germany, late May 1945. Awards presentation. Lieutenant General Anders presents Lieutenant General Simonds the order of the Virtuti Militari (silver cross) with General Crocker to Simonds right. Other officers unidentified.

233. Jever, Germany, late May 1945. Lieutenant General Anders inspects the Division followed by left to right, Lieutenant General Simonds, General Crocker and Major General Maczek. On the far right, the Officer saluting is Lieutenant Jerzy Niewinowski, recipient of the Order of the Virtuti Militari Class V – Silver Cross. On 21 August 1944, Officer Cadet Niewinowski, commanding a three tank reconnaissance patrol, made contact with the Canadian relief force advancing towards the surrounded forces of the Division defending Mount Ormel, 'Falaise Pocket', Normandy.

234. Jever, Germany, late May 1945. Liberated Polish prisoners including women from the Armia Krajowa (Home Army) wait to greet General Anders. Originally captured during the Warsaw Uprising in August-October 1944, the women were liberated by the Division on 12 April 1945 from Stalag VI C, Oberlangen, Germany.

Part IV

1945–47

235. Beveren-Waas, Belgium, 2 March 1946 (sequential photos 235–241). Following the town's liberation by 2nd Armoured Regiment, its coat of arms were presented, along with the colours by General Klemens Rudnicki (1897–1992) Divisional commander, who had succeeded General Maczek (extreme right) in late May 1945. Rudnicki is seen here accepting the colour from the town's mayor, with third from left, Colonel Grudziński and Colonel Majewski immediately behind the mayor.

236. Beveren-Waas, Belgium, 2 March 1946. The Regimental Guard of Honour in the town square. Note the town's coat of arms in the form of a shield, worn below the Poland shoulder title on the right sleeve of the soldier, second from right.

237. Beveren-Waas, Belgium, 2 March 1946. Major Michał Gutowski (CO 2nd Armoured Regiment) prepares to accept the colour from General Rudnicki. Having served in the Austro-Hungarian army in the First World War, Rudnicki joined the Polish army and fought in the Polish-Bolshevik War 1919–1920 as a cavalry commander. During the campaign of 1939 he commanded 9th Lancers and was taken prisoner by the Soviets. Escaping, he became active within the resistance, rising to command the movement within the Soviet-occupied zone of Poland. He was re-captured, endured imprisonment and interrogation but without declaring his rank and was eventually freed following the German invasion in June 1941. Along with Anders and his men, he was evacuated to the Middle East where 2nd Corps was created. The Corps campaigned in Italy from December 1943 until the German surrender on 2nd May 1945, acting as the deputy commander of 5th Kresowa (Eastern Poland) Infantry Division until his appointment on 21 May 1945 as commander of the 1st Polish Armoured Division in occupied Germany. Following his discharge he lived in exile in London.

238. Beveren-Waas, Belgium, 2 March 1946. Major Gutowski, CO, 2nd Armoured Regiment, leads the colour party pass the crowds in the town square with Warrant Officer First Class (WO1) Aleksander Jarzembowski carrying the standard.

239. Beveren-Waas, Belgium, 2 March 1946. The Divisional Band marches into the square to take position opposite the rostrum.

240. Beveren-Waas, Belgium, 2 March 1946. General Rudnicki (to the right of the civilian) is greeted by local dignitaries and Belgium officers, prior to a regimental parade. Below the rostrum, the colour party awaits the march-past. The standard bearer is Warrant Officer First Class (WO1) Aleksander Leon Jarzembowski with on his right, Lieutenant Jerzy Niewinowski.

241. Beveren-Waas, Belgium, 2 March 1946. General Rudnicki salutes the Regimental march-past.

242. Constitution Day, Divisional parade, Meppen, Germany, 3 May 1946. Sherman MkIIA with the colours of 2nd Armoured Regiment. On the right, holding the standard is Warrant Officer First Class (WO1) Alexsander Jarzembowski with Lieutenant Jerzy Niewinowski on the left.

243. Divisional parade, Meppen, Germany 3 May 1946. Regimental Colour parties form up prior to a mass held on a temporary altar to celebrate the declaration of the Constitution (3 May 1791) during the Polish – Lithuanian Commonwealth.

244. Regimental parade, Herzlake, Germany, 8 August 1946 (sequential photos 244–249). The Divisional band lead the way for the Colour Party and the Guard of Honour, passing several Stuart tanks covered in tarpaulins, on their way to the ceremonial area.

245. The Colour Party of 2nd Armoured Regiment. The standard bearer is Warrant Officer First Class (WO1) Aleksander Leon Jarzembowski.

246. The Colour Party wheel their way past Shermans, covered with all-weather tarpaulins.

247. Entering the ceremonial area, the the column marches pass General Rudnicki, who can be seen taking the salute under the Polish flag on the left. An altar has been built, draped over with the Polish flag mounting a Polish eagle, surround by two large Divisional pennons (black and orange with a central thin white stripe) and topped with the honorary insignia of the coat of arms of Bevern-Waas. Four Sherman tanks are positioned, flanking the altar with supports displaying the National flag.

248. A mass is conducted for the regiment, supported by the Divisonal band. The Sherman Mk IIAs are all covered in a very well organised layer of add-on armour made up of Sherman tracks welded onto the tank. Under battlefield conditions the application was more haphazard with tracks often used from both a variety of Allied and German armour. Note that the Divisional signs are painted onto removable tin plates, clipped onto the welded-on tracks. On the barrels can be seen the fading remains of the 'trompe l'oeil', white camouflage paint, used to confuse the barrel length.

249. General Rudnicki inspects the Colour Party and the Guard of Honour.

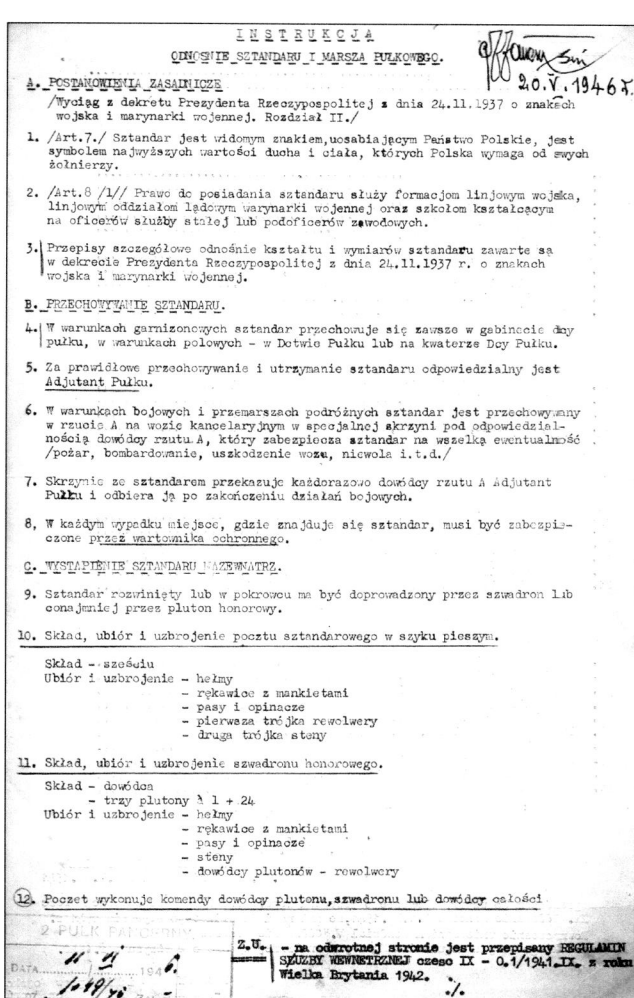

250. Instructions and procedures for the Regimental Flag and Regimental March, printed 1942, re-stamped 1946. Issued to 2nd Armoured Regiment.

251. Bad Bentheim, Lower Saxony, Germany circa 1946–47 (sequential photos 251–254). M10 Achilles of 2nd Battery, 1st Anti-Tank Artillery Regiment parade through the streets prior to a ceremony in Bentheim Castle. Note welded on tank tracks for additional armoured protection. The Regimental tactical sign, a white 77 on a red over blue square, is seen on the left trackguard with the Divisional marking on the lower hull, painted against a white oblong background. (Richard Szczawinski)

252. Bad Bentheim, Lower Saxony, Germany circa 1946–47. Another photo of the parade in photo (251). A half-track tows a 17 pounder anti-tank gun, which appears to be draped in a camouflage net. (Richard Szczawinski)

253. Bentheim Castle, Lower Saxony, Germany circa 1946–47. General Maczek, dressed in his favoured 1938 issue black leather coat, presents the colours of 1st Anti-Tank Artillery Regiment at a ceremony within the castle courtyard. Immediately behind stands General Rudnicki. (Richard Szczawinski)

254. Bentheim Castle, Lower Saxony, Germany circa 1946–47. A mass is held as part of the ceremony within the courtyard with General Maczek and other officers seated in front of the altar. A band is present in the top right-hand corner. Note that the soldiers appear to be wearing the 1944 Mark III 'Turtle' helmet as well as the Tankers helmet. (Richard Szczawinski)

255–256. Divisional Headquarters, Meppen, Germany 1947. The colours of 2nd Armoured Regiment carried by Warrant Officer First Class (WO1) Aleksander Leon Jarzembowski, are presented to General Gwilym Ivor Thomas (1893–1972) escorted by General Klemens Rudnicki. Thomas commanded the 43rd (Wessex) Division 1942–45, followed by 1 Corps District, British Army Of the Rhine (BAOR) 1945–47 and then administrator for Polish Forces under British Command in 1947.

PART IV: 1945–47   141

257–258. Polish Resettlement Corps (1946–1949). Examples of documentation used by the PRC. Formed by the British government to help exiled Poles adjust to civilian life and included teaching of the language and new skills to enable employment.

```
ON HIS MAJESTY'S SERVICE                    OFFICIAL PAID

                    The Officer i/c P.R. Corps Records,
                              at WITLEY CAMP,
                                  GODALMING,
                                        SURREY
        THE WAR OFFICE        DISCHARGED


                THIRD FOLD HERE
        W TYM MIEJSCU-TRZECIE ZAGIĘCIE

        ON HIS MAJESTY'S SERVICE

        THE OFFICER IN CHARGE,
        Polish Resettlement Corps Records,
                Witley Camp,
                Nr. Godalming,
                        Surrey
```

```
        THE GOVERNMENT GRANT IN AID OF POLISH EX-SERVICEMEN IN U.K.

    Imię i nazwisko (Full name): ..........................................
    Pełny adres (Full address): ..........................................
              ..........................................
    Data urodzenia (Date of Birth): ..........................................
    Stan rodzinny (single, married, widowed): ..........................
    Stopień wojskowy (Rank): .............. PKPR (PRC) No..............
    Ostatni przydział w W.P. (last Unit in Pol.Forces): ................
    Typ mieszkania - dom,pokoje itp.(Type of accommod.- house,flat,room etc.)
              ..........................................
    Dane odnośnie członków rodziny i osób zamieszkałych z petentem (Parti-
    culars of members of the family or other persons sharing Applicant's
    accommodations):

    ─────────────────────────────────────────────────────────────────────
    Imię i nazwisko   : Data urodz. : Pokrewieństwo : Zajęcie  : Zarobek
    (Name and surname): (Date of    : (Relationship): (Occu-   : tygodn.
                      :  birth)     :               :  pation) : (Earnings
                      :             :               :          :  weekly)
    ─────────────────────────────────────────────────────────────────────
                      :             :               :          :
    ─────────────────────────────────────────────────────────────────────
                      :             :               :          :
    ─────────────────────────────────────────────────────────────────────
                      :             :               :          :
    ─────────────────────────────────────────────────────────────────────

                TYGODNIOWY DOCHOD - (WEEKLY EARNINGS)

    Emerytura petenta (Applicant's Retirement pension) ......... £......
```

259. General Anders, late 1960s, London. While Anders addresses the audience, Polish veterans stand with their Colours at the rear of the stage. Warrant Officer First Class (WO1) Aleksander Leon Jarzembowski, 2nd Armoured Regiment, can be seen fifth from the right. Anders remained in exile taking an active role in the Polish Government-in-exile. Following his death on 12 May 1970, he was buried with his soldiers at the Polish military cemetery at Monte Cassino, the scene of his greatest achievement in the Italian Campaign.

260. Royal Albert Hall, London, 28 September 1969.
Colour bearers, prior to being summoned onstage at a post war ceremony, with on the left, Warrant Officer First Class (WO1) Aleksander Leon Jarzembowski followed by an unknown sergeant of 3rd Carpathian Rifle Division, 2nd Polish Corps. Old soldiers never die, they just fade away... .

Appendix

Order Of Battle 1st Polish Armoured Division North-West Europe 1944–45

Divisional Headquarters and Divisional Support
10th Mounted Rifle Regiment (Reconnaissance)
Traffic Control Squadron, Field Court, Field Post Office, Quartermaster, Chaplain, Provost, Field Security, Paymaster, 1st Forward Tank Delivery Squadron, 10th Mounted Rifle Regiment

Armoured Brigade – 10th Armoured Cavalry Brigade
HQ
1st Armoured Regiment
2nd Armoured Regiment
24th Lancers Regiment
10th Dragoons Regiment

Infantry Brigade – 3rd Rifle Brigade
HQ
1st Podhale (Highland) Rifle Battalion
8th Rifle Battalion
9th Rifle Battalion
1st Independent Heavy Machine-Gun Squadron

Divisional Artillery
HQ
1st Motorised Artillery Regiment (Self-Propelled)
2nd Motorised Artillery Regiment (Towed)
1st Anti-Tank Artillery Regiment
1st Anti-Aircraft Artillery Regiment

Divisional Engineers
HQ
10th Field Company Engineers
11th Field Company Engineers
Field Park Company
Bridge Platoon

Divisional Signals - 1st Signals Battalion
HQ Squadron
1st, 2nd, 3rd, 10th Signals Squadrons

Divisional Workshops
3rd and 10th Workshop Companies

Divisional Medical Units
10th Light Field Ambulance
11th Heavy Field Ambulance
1st Field Dressing Station
1st Field Hygiene Station

Divisonal Supply Units
3rd Transport Company (Ammunition)
10th Transport Company (Petrol)
11th Transport Company (Rations)
Infantry Transport Company

Bibliography

CORRESPONDENCE
David Bradley
Tony Colvin
Dr. Jens Graul
Evan McGilvray
Kuba Jarzembowski
Kazik Jarzembowski
Zygmunt Kopel
David Paintin
Richard Szczawinski
Ken Tout
Jacques Van-Dijke

BOOKS & ARTICLES
Barbarski, Krzysztof, *Polish Armour 1939–45*. Osprey Vanguard number 30, Osprey Publishing, London, 1982.
1st Polish Armoured Division (1 VIII 1944 – 11 XI 1944) France-Belgium-Holland. Louis Vermijs N.V., Breda-Osterhout, n.d.
Colvin, Tony, "Wilhelmshaven", *After the Battle* Number 148. Battle of Britain International Ltd, Harlow, 2010.
Higgins, David R, *Panzer II vs 7TP: Poland 1939*. Osprey Duel number 66, Osprey Publishing, Oxford, 2015.
Jamar, K, *With the Tanks of the 1st Polish Armoured Division*. H.L.Smit & ZN, Hengelo, 1946.
Jackowski, Grzegorz, *Wozy bojowe Wojska Polskiego 1939*. Wydawnictwo "Militaria", Warszawa, 2012.
Jarzembowski, Jan & Bradley, David, *Armoured Hussars 2. Images of the 1st Polish Armoured Division, Normandy, August 1944*. Helion & Company, Solihull, 2015.
Kaminski, Andrzej Antoni, *Od " Acromy " do " Zwyciezcy*. Malopolska Poligrafia, Krakow.
Kuchanski, Halik, *The Eagle Unbowed, Poland and the Poles in the Second World War*.
Allen Lane, London, 2012.
Lalak, Zbigniew, *Lexicon of World War II Armed Forces vol.1, Polish Armoured Forces 1939–1945, Organisation and Order Of Battle*. Warsaw, Pegaz-Bis / O.K! MEDIA, n.d.
Majka, Jerzy, *Invincible Black Brigade, Polish 10th Cavalry Brigade 1939*, Green Series No 4107. Mushroom Model Publications, Sandomierz, 2010.
McGilvray, Evan, *The Black Devils' March, A Doomed Odyssey – The 1st Polish Armoured Division 1939–45*. Helion & Company, Solihull, 2005.
McGilvray, Evan, *Man of Steel and Honour-General Stanislaw Maczek, Soldier of Poland, Commander of the 1st Polish Armoured Division in North-West Europe 1944–45*. Helion & Company, Solihull, 2012.
Mieczkowski, Zbigniew, *The Soldiers of General Maczek in World War II*, Foundation for the Commemoration of General Maczek First Polish Armoured Division,Warsaw, 2004.
Prenatt, Jamie, *Polish Armor of the Blitzkrieg*. Osprey New Vanguard number 224, Osprey Publishing, Oxford, 2015.
Wiatrowski, Tadeusz, *2nd Polish Armoured Regiment in Action, From Caen to Wilhelmshaven*. Schlutersche Buchdruckerei, Hannover, 1946.

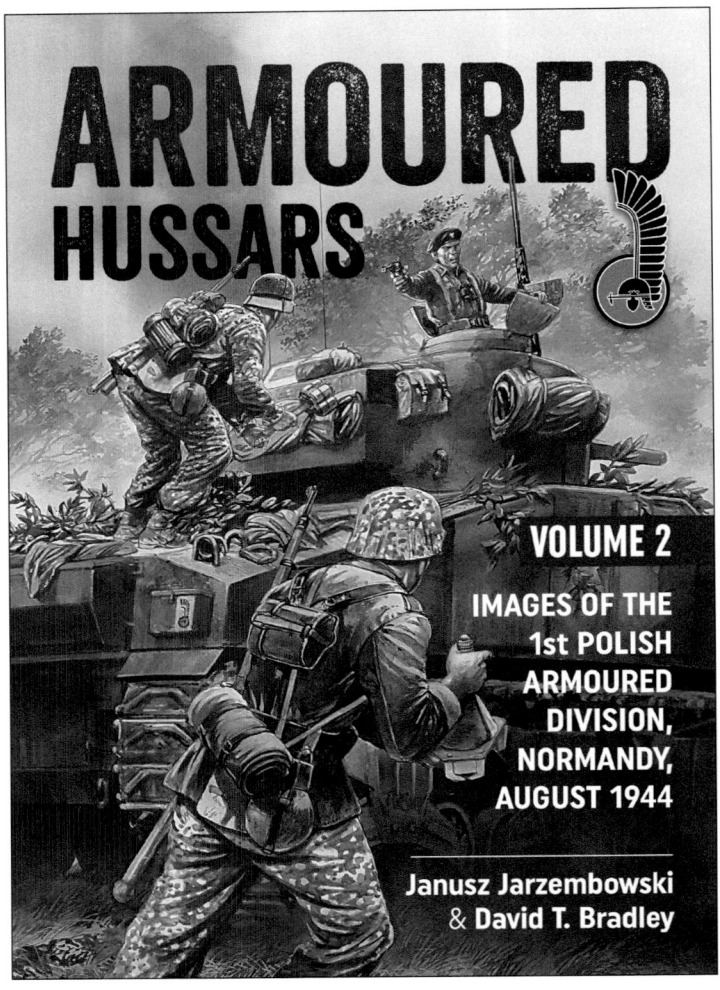

Armoured Hussars Volume 2
Images of the 1st Polish Armoured Division, Normandy, August 1944

Janusz Jarzembowski & David T. Bradley

ISBN 9781910777237 (paperback)

Armoured Hussars Volume 2 provides a highly-illustrated account of the 1st Polish Armoured Division's baptism of fire in Normandy in August 1944, from Operations Totalise and Tractable to the victory at Falaise, culminating at the climactic battle on Mont Ormel - the site of this triumph was justly named A Polish Battlefield by the Canadians. This album contains contributions written by the distinguished military author and Normandy veteran Ken Tout, who was recently awarded the Knight's Cross of the Order of Merit by the Republic of Poland for popularising the Polish soldiers of the Second World War. Serving as a young Sherman tank crewman in the Northamptonshire Yeomanry, Ken watched the Poles go in to action on 8 August and witnessed their savage baptism of fire. The album features many dramatic photographs and documents, numbering over 250, from the renowned Polish Institute and Sikorski Museum (PISM) as well as from the author's collection. It is also supplemented by eight pages of colour plates featuring divisional armour, uniforms, maps and a centre page-spread of a close-quarter action on Mont Ormel, based on the memoirs of a regimental commander. Illustrated by the renowned military artist, Peter Dennis, this depiction also features on the front cover. This book will appeal to all who have an interest in the Second World War and the Normandy Campaign, and is a fitting tribute to those Polish soldiers who fought so gallantly for Europe's freedom as part of the Allied Liberation Army and played a decisive role in the defeat of German forces in France at the Battle of the Falaise Pocket in August 1944